Life in Stuart London

*The Lord Mayor and the Court of Aldermen,
with the arms of the City of London centre-
front. Frontispiece to the 'Present State of
London' by T. de Laune, 1690.*

Life in Stuart London

Peggy Miller

*Illustrated with photographs
and with drawings
by Gabrielle Stoddart*

METHUEN · LONDON

Acknowledgements

Permission to reproduce illustrations is gratefully acknowledged to Aerofilms for that on page 35; Cambridge University Library for the frontispiece to this book and that on page 89; Department of the Environment for those on pages 10, 13 which are Crown Copyright reproduced with permission of The Controller of Her Majesty's Stationery Office, and that on page 43 which is reproduced by permission of the Admiral President, Royal Naval College, Greenwich; Dulwich College Gallery for that on page 17; Guildhall Library for those on pages 16, 19, 45; Greater London Council and The London Fire Brigade for that on page 58; Historical Picture Service for those on pages 11, 18, 23, 56, 67, 78 and 86; the Victoria and Albert Museum 84; the National Portrait Gallery for those on pages 8, 12, 21, 26, 33, 39, 53, 63, 69, 76 and 79; the Radio Times Hulton Picture Library for that on pages 60/61; the Society of Antiquaries for those on pages 27, 37 and 55; the Trustees of the British Museum for those on pages 11, 18, 23, 56, 67, 78 and 86; the Victoria and Albert Museum for those on pages 4, 48/49, 65, 68 and 73; the Worshipful Company of Mercers for that on page 42. The illustration on page 14 is reproduced by Gracious Permission of Her Majesty the Queen.

The cover illustration is 'Frost Fair on the Thames' by Abraham Hondius and is reproduced by kind permission of the Museum of London.

Uniform with this volume

LIFE IN ELIZABETHAN LONDON
by Peggy Miller

First published in Great Britain 1977 by
Methuen Children's Books Ltd
11 New Fetter Lane, London EC4P 4EE
Text copyright © 1977 by Peggy Miller
Drawings copyright © 1977
by Methuen Children's Books Ltd
Filmset by Keyspools Ltd
Golborne, Lancashire
Printed in Great Britain
by Butler & Tanner Ltd, Frome and London

ISBN 0 416 80190 0

Contents

1   The effects of the Stuarts on London   *page* 7

2   Plague and fire   22

3   Rebuilding the City   38

4   The development of London   47

5   London's 'new look'   62

6   Domestic life and leisure   72

7   'The Spirit of the Age'   83

Select Bibliography   93

Index   94

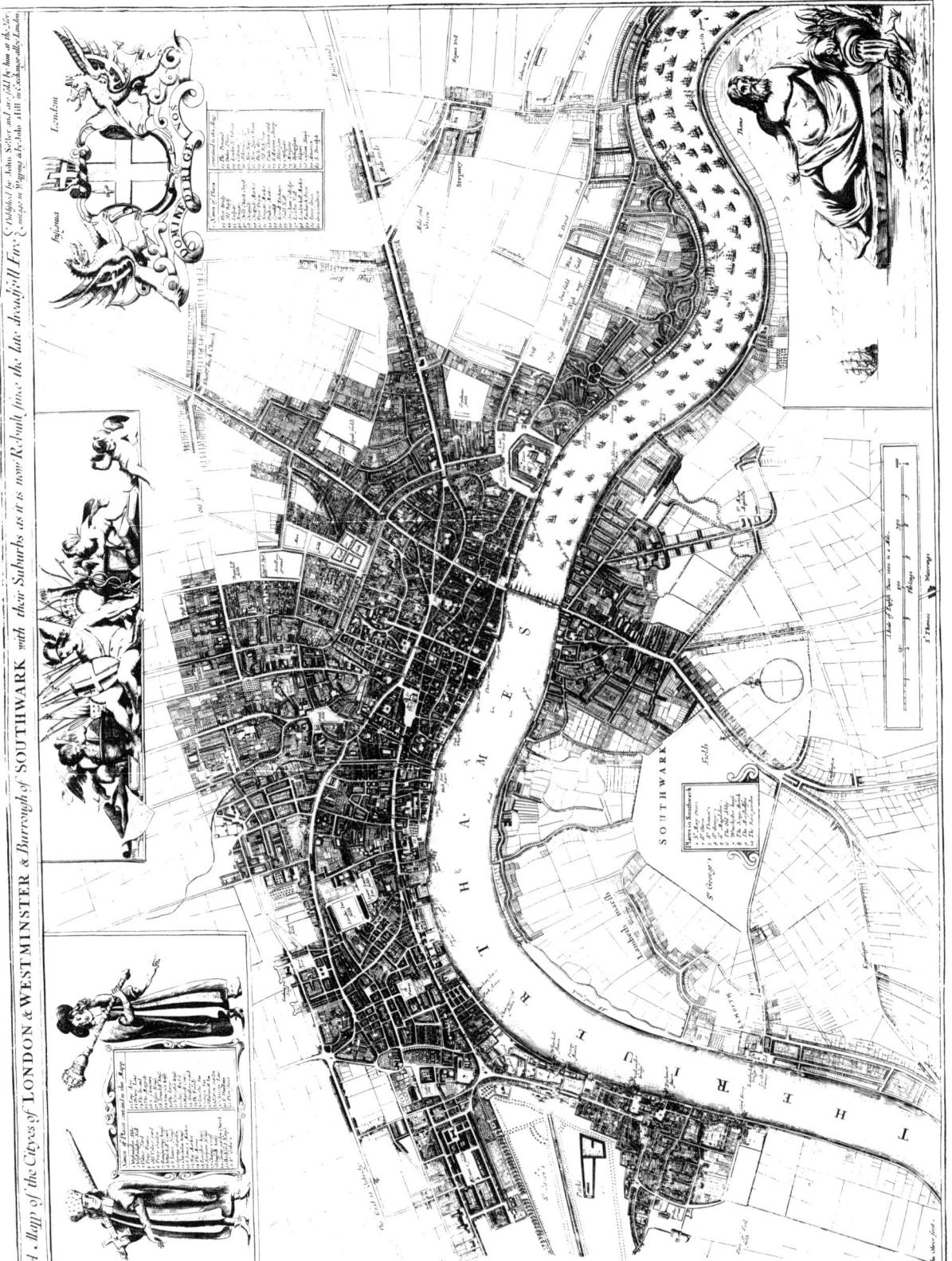

London after the Great Fire of 1666.

I
The effects
of the
Stuarts on London

Looking back in time, we can see that a most remarkable change in London's size and appearance took place during the seventeenth century. And we can trace the reason for the beginning of that change as far back as the end of the reign of Queen Elizabeth I. In 1598 the elderly antiquarian, John Stow, published his *Survey of London*, a sort of combined history and guidebook which was the first of its kind.

INIGO JONES

In the same year of 1598 young Lord Roos decided to take a journey through France, Germany and Italy. With him went a young painter, Inigo Jones, whose eyes were opened to the glory of Italy and in particular to the work of its greatest architect, Andrea Palladio. Palladio's life stretched across most of the sixteenth century, and his great aim was to revive the beauty and majesty of classic architecture in Italy. He built stately houses and beautiful churches in Rome, Venice and Vicenza – the setting for his last and perhaps most famous work, the Olympico Theatre. But lacking the money to build in stone or

Inigo Jones, 1573–1652, the first of our great architects, who brought the Palladian style to England. His life spanned the reigns of Elizabeth I, James I and Charles I as well as Cromwell's Commonwealth. Portrait after Vandyck.

marble, Palladio usually made his buildings out of brick faced with a kind of plaster known as stucco, and they did not last. Here and there a church, such as San Giorgio Maggiore in Venice, or a house, such as the Villa Capra in Vicenza, or the theatre – the Teatro Olimpico – remain. Much more was to be seen still standing when Jones visited Italy, and Palladio's work became his greatest source of inspiration.

Little is known of Inigo Jones's history, but the few facts we do have seem to indicate that he was born the son of a clothmaker in the parish of St Bartholomew the Great in London where he was baptised on 19 July 1573. He lived through the reigns of the first two Stuart kings, James I (1603–1625) and Charles I (1625–1649) and died in Cromwell's Commonwealth in 1652.

Lord Roos's tour lasted three years, and Jones seems to have become proficient in French and Italian, which was to stand him in good stead later. In 1603 he went abroad again, this time with Lord Roos's brother, the Earl of Rutland, and seems to have become known to the Danish court, for in the following year he returned to London to enter the service of the Queen, Anne of Denmark.

Queen Anne was already well launched on a career of expensive frivolity. She loved masques, costly entertainments performed in gorgeous costumes by the ladies and gentlemen of the court against beautiful backgrounds and scenery which sometimes involved the use of quite complicated machinery. There were transformation scenes and gods and godesses flew across the skies suspended on wires; there were

Anne of Denmark, who married King James I in 1589, and was a great enthusiast for masques, many of which were designed by Inigo Jones. Painting attributed to W. Larkin.

songs and ballets, and the performers were selected as much for their looks as for their acting ability. Altogether the masque was the Jacobean equivalent of a musical 'spectacular' today. Mostly the stories were slight, but they were told in stately verse and were usually based on Greek legends or other ancient myths extolling the glories of kingship. The Queen took part in these entertainments, often playing the most important role.

Inigo Jones produced many of the designs for the costumes and scenery and became famous for them; a number of his exquisitely drawn designs still exist. In 1605 he collaborated with Ben Jonson, who wrote the verse, in *The Masque of Blackness and of Beauty*, which was performed on Twelfth Night, with the Queen and her ladies made up as blackamoors.

In 1608 Jones designed a masque for the Earl of Salisbury. It so happened that, in the same year, the Earl had bought a strip of land which had previously belonged to Durham House, one of the palaces built with an entry on the Strand and with gardens running down to the Thames at the back. The Earl was one of the first building speculators, if not the first, and he proposed to turn this expensive plot into a building and shopping centre similar to the one built in 1567 by Sir Thomas Gresham in Cornhill – the Royal Exchange. Jones designed the New Exchange, or Britain's Burse as it was to be called. And although neither this nor his drawing for the completion of the central

The first Royal Exchange in Cornhill founded by Sir Thomas Gresham in 1566 and visited by Queen Elizabeth I in 1571.

nave of St Paul's was used, it marked the turning-point for Jones as an architect, although he was still very much in demand for staging masques.

With Palladio as his example, Jones designed buildings in a majestic, classical style, with flat slab fronts and large windows, in contrast to the informal and irregular buildings of the London of the Tudors which was built piecemeal and without any regard for the planning of a street. The great difference between Jones's designs and Tudor building was that his vision of London was one of brick and stone, whereas the city that existed then was built mainly from wood, lathe and plaster on brick foundations.

Jones became Surveyor (a kind of chief architect and builder-adviser) to Henry, Prince of Wales, in 1611, and then returned to Italy

An early masterpiece by Inigo Jones: the Banqueting House, Whitehall, built between 1619 and 1622. This is all that now remains of the vast palace of Whitehall. It was refaced with Portland stone in 1829, and the original mullion windows have been changed to sashes. Charles I was executed on a scaffold placed on a level with the first-floor windows in 1649.

Aula Domus Arrundeliana, Londini, Meridiem versus,

The south aspect of Arundel House, London, in 1646. Etched by Wenceslas Hollar.

in the suite of the Earl of Arundel in 1613. He was in Italy two years and, on his return to London, was made the Royal Surveyor of Works.

COVENT GARDEN

The most remarkable innovation of Jones was the *piazza* he built in Covent Garden: this was to alter the course of all future building in London. A royal commission had been set up in 1625, with Inigo Jones as one of its members, to see that no more new building was carried out except on old foundations. Nevertheless, Francis Russell, fourth Earl of Bedford, found ways of getting round this prohibition, and obtained a licence in 1631 for the building of houses 'fit for the habitacions of Gentlemen and men of ability' in the area known as Covent Garden which had once been the Convent Garden of the Abbey of Westminster. He also obtained Inigo Jones as his architect.

Jones designed something which had never been seen before. He built the first London square. On the west side he placed the Church of St Paul's, Covent Garden, which, repaired and restored, still stands today. The Earl did not want to spend much money on the church – after all he was a speculator! – so he gave Jones £5000 and told him that he did not want anything more elaborate than a big barn. 'You shall have the handsomest barn in England,' Jones is said to have replied. And this is what he built. It was a plain, rectangular, but majestic building, reminiscent of a primitive Greek temple, its pediment

11

Prince Henry, eldest son of
James I, who died suddenly,
aged eighteen, in 1612.
Painted by R. Peake.

supported on pillars. It faced the houses on the east side of the square across an open space with freshly planted trees and a sundial in the centre. There were houses on the north side as well, but the south side was taken up by the garden wall of Bedford House which belonged to the Earl.

The extraordinary thing to the Londoners, who were used to the projecting gables, black and white timber and plaster, small mullioned windows and higgledy-piggledy 'design', was that those houses were built of brick, and brick covered with stucco, which gave the semblance of stone, in four orderly blocks on two sides of the square. Their street entrances opened on to pillared and vaulted arcades providing protection from rain or sun. The backs of the houses gave on to gardens and mews for stabling.

The famous diarist, John Evelyn, said that it reminded him of a square in Leghorn which Jones had undoubtedly seen during his sojourns in Italy, and it also looked something like the rue Royale in Paris. The houses were expensive and were sought after by the richer Londoners, but streets began to extend from them on the east and south, and the houses in these were slightly less costly. They were not all designed by Jones, but he had the supervision of their appearance in his capacity as the Royal Surveyor of Works.

The square in the middle was originally intended to provide a pleasant place for people to walk or sit in, as painted benches had been provided for that purpose, but the Earl, who seems to have been a good businessman, began a fruit and vegetable market along his garden wall with the produce from his garden. Gradually, this extended into the centre of the *piazza* but, as it grew more noisy and crowded, so the nobility moved out west or north into the countryside of Kensington and Bloomsbury. None of the houses of the *piazza* remains today, but

The Queen's House, Greenwich, begun by Inigo Jones in 1617 for Anne of Denmark, queen of James I, and finished for her daughter-in-law, Henrietta Maria, in 1635. It now forms the central part of the National Maritime Museum.

Interior of The Queen's Chapel at St James built by Inigo Jones for the Spanish Infanta, the intended bride of Prince Charles in 1623, but completed for the French princess Henrietta Maria whom, as king, he married in 1625.

the church, which was burned down in 1790 and rebuilt to Jones's original plan, still exists. The market has lasted until the nineteen-seventies.

BUILDINGS BY INIGO JONES

Few of Inigo Jones's buildings in or around London remain today. He built the Queen's House at Greenwich in the grounds of the Palace, as a separate dwelling for Queen Anne, but it was not finished until the next reign when Henrietta Maria was queen to Charles I. It is beautiful in its complete simplicity. The Banqueting House in Whitehall, with a magnificent ceiling, by Rubens commissioned by Charles I to the memory of his father, James I, can still be admired today, as can the Queen's Chapel in St James's Palace. This chapel was originally intended for the use of the Spanish Infanta whom Prince Charles first intended to marry, but it was finished in time for Charles's marriage, as King, to the French princess, Henrietta Maria, in 1625.

Architect though he was, Jones was not above designing a gateway here or a stone lantern for a hall there, and two isolated pieces of his design remain in the watergate he created for the Duke of Buckingham's residence, York House, and another gateway for Beaufort House. York House has long since disappeared and the Thames has receded yards from where it first lapped at the stone steps. Likewise, Beaufort House is no longer, but the gateway was given in the next century to the Earl of Burlington, a great admirer of Palladio and of Jones, and he erected it in the gardens surrounding his Palladian villa at Chiswick.

Apart from the Covent Garden Piazza and the surrounding streets, as well as one or two buildings – the Banqueting House and St Paul's Cathedral's west front, for instance – the influence of Inigo Jones, the first strongly marked foreign influence on the appearance of London, did not affect the city very much as a whole at that time. It was only later, after the second of the two great disasters London was to suffer in the seventeenth century – the Plague and the Great Fire – that it was recognized.

JAMES I

When James I rode into his capital from Scotland in 1603, he looked on London and liked what he saw. To him it meant the richest capital and the most thriving commercial centre in Europe, but not much more. Elizabeth I (1558–1603) had had a love and respect for London: she was, after all, a great-granddaughter of a Lord Mayor of London, and the people of London loved her. But James rode in almost as a foreigner; it was not to be expected that he would have the same high regard for the city and its citizens as the old Queen had possessed.

During the reign of the Stuarts the City of London reached its highest point of political importance but, at the same time, its ties with the Crown began to loosen. Even in Elizabeth's reign, with the exception of a small group of the nobility who were concerned with poetry, the theatre and, to a lesser degree, with music, and who were friendly with poets, playwrights, actors and musicians, there had been divisions between the aristocratic, wealthy class and the merchants and working class. But each had had a healthy respect for the other, and there was a simplicity in their dealings with each other. Every man knew his place in life, and if a merchant, by clever but honest dealing, managed to marry his daughter into a noble line, he was not sneered at

any more than a successful merchant despised a hardworking journeyman who had managed to save up enough for a shop of his own. And the people of London knew that they always had recourse to the Queen through their Lord Mayor and Aldermen against any abuse by the nobility. The Lord Mayor was second only to the monarch in the City, and the monarch only entered there with his permission.

JAMES I WOOS THE CITY

James I knew that he had to woo the City to some degree if he wanted their support and particularly if he wanted to borrow money from them, so he joined the Company of Clothmakers. There was some justice in this because James always had a morbid fear of assassination and wore all his clothes heavily padded and quilted so that they should prove a shield against a dagger or sword point. Consequently he wore far more material in his suits than most other gentlemen in London. His son, Prince Henry, the Prince of Wales, who was to die before he could come to the throne, joined the Merchant Taylors' Company.

Although the Stuart kings frequently asked for loans from the City, their attitudes towards it were on the whole often very disdainful, if not contemptuous. In spite of James's attempts to join the merchants, from

*King James I
(1603–1625) by Marc
Ghaeraedts. Note the
padded effect of the doublet
and hose in accordance with
James's idea of protection
against an assassin's
dagger.*

the time of his accession onwards, the division between the sovereign and the citizens of London became more marked.

During Elizabeth's reign a great number of her courtiers had lived in the City – Sir Francis Drake, for example, had lived in Thames Street, one of the busiest and noisiest streets in the City. When the King kept more and more to his Palace of Whitehall, there seemed to be fewer royal progresses into the City itself, and many of the nobility began to move westwards. Apart from this, the growth of small industries within the one square mile of London and the attendant smoke and smell was beginning to make it a less inviting place to live in. So the nobility moved out – to Covent Garden, Bloomsbury, Kensington and Westminster. The rich merchants, however, still remained in their houses in the City. When the King and Court withdrew from London they left behind the beginnings of class distinction.

THE NEW RIVER

Perhaps the most practical thing James did for London was to help with the supply of fresh water to the City. The waterwheel which had been built in 1581 by the Dutchman Peter Morrice at the first arch of London Bridge still functioned perfectly, but it could supply only a limited

Sir Hugh Myddleton, born about 1560, who was responsible for the channelling of the New River circa 1613, and for organizing London's water supply. Engraving after Cornelius Johnson.

area from the bridge. In 1605 Parliament passed an act authorising water to be brought down in pipes or brick trenches from Hertfordshire in the north. The first two attempts were unsuccessful, and then Hugh Myddleton, a wealthy goldsmith, said that he would pay for the work to be carried out. But he was hampered in it by people through whose land the pipes had to run, and a great deal of sabotage went on. Feelings ran high about the pipe installation in much the same way as they do today when it is proposed to build a new motorway or airport across private property. Finally, Myddleton appealed to the King, and James decided to pay half the costs himself and take half the profits. A canal about ten feet wide and four feet deep was dug out and wooden pipes carried the water for thirty-eight miles to and across London. There were originally about 800 bridges over this canal which was known as the New River, and it gave London several million gallons of water a day. This was the beginning of London's water supply as we know it, and we have to thank the first of the Stuarts and a goldsmith for it.

In the next reign, relations between Charles I and London became strained and the City took the side of Parliament for the most part. The disruption of industry and commerce meant that the City had very little money, but that did not prevent Charles calling upon it for a loan after he had dissolved Parliament for not granting the money. London gave him £20 000, which it could ill spare. In 1627 he asked for another loan and, after protest, the City gave him £120 000 which was to aid him in his war with France. Some of the Aldermen were sent to prison for refusing the loan.

Charles's favourite, the Duke of Buckingham, had long displeased the Londoners by his insolence and heedless extravagance. They held him responsible for leading the King into war with France and, when he was assassinated in 1628, they welcomed the event. They equally resented William Laud whom Charles made Bishop of London. Nine-tenths of Londoners were Puritans, and they were offended by Laud's use of High Church rites and ceremonies. In 1621 a hundred and two Puritans had left Plymouth to found the first colony in America and there were many Londoners among them. In 1635 another 4890 people left for America seeking freedom of worship.

LONDON AND THE CIVIL WAR

Charles imposed crippling taxes upon the City, the most infamous of which was Ship Money. This meant that the City had to produce the money for seven ships of 4000 tons and 1560 men, and it was one of the causes leading to the Civil War (1642–1646). London, for the most part, took the side of Parliament. Relations between the King and Parliament became more and more strained until he took the rash step of entering the House of Commons uninvited and demanding the delivery unto him of five Members of Parliament, whereupon the City sheltered the five, and Londoners shouted abuse to the King when he came into the City seeking them.

With the outbreak of the war, the King recognized the fact that he could not count upon the capital, so the seat of government was eventually moved to Oxford. The City raised £100 000 for Parliament at the beginning of the war and supplied further money later, as well as the trained bands of the London militia. The war weighed heavily upon the Londoners: lodging-keepers in the Strand were ruined, bankruptcy was everywhere, there was no business transacted on the Royal Exchange and no trade in the shops.

In spite of all this, many of them were stricken as they watched from behind the lines of helmeted soldiers the slight, dignified figure of the King walk from St James's Palace through the Park and Spring Garden to Whitehall on a bleak January morning in 1649. He passed through the splendours of Inigo Jones's Banqueting House with its magnificent Rubens ceiling, for the last time, and stepped out on to the black-shrouded scaffold where his executioners awaited him.

King Charles I (1625–1649) with the symbols of royal power; the crown, orb and sceptre, by his hand. Painted by Daniel Muytens.

2
Plague
and fire

A T THIS time there was very little difference in the shape of Elizabethan London and that of the seventeenth century: it stretched from Clerkenwell in the north to the Thames in the south, from the Strand in the west to the Tower in the east. But the city walls gradually fell into disrepair and the green fields, which were once found here and there within the City, had by now completely vanished and were built over.

When any of the old houses fell down, which they did fairly frequently, they were rebuilt without the projecting upper storeys and with tiles instead of thatch. No more great mansions were built and only half a dozen or so nobles still retained their houses within the City limits, although all the great merchants remained loyal to the place which had helped to provide their wealth.

LONDON UNDER CROMWELL

Nothing in the City's appearance was altered much during Cromwell's Protectorate, but all joy had been killed. Music-making, except for psalm-singing, was frowned upon, and gaiety vanished from the

London during the Fire, 1666.

London streets. Most of the old festivals were banned; Mayday and the Maypole were no more, and saints' days were not observed.

All theatres were closed, and many of the actors joined the Cavaliers and fought for the King. The Globe Theatre was pulled down in 1642; the Rose, Swan and the Bear Garden had disappeared before that. In 1649 the Fortune Theatre was destroyed by soldiers and the Blackfriars was also pulled down in 1655, after standing empty for some years.

If London was basically the same in appearance as it had been in James's time, it was mainly because Cromwell had enforced the rules prohibiting building on new sites within ten miles of the walls. But shortly after the Restoration of Charles II, it was to experience the most dramatic period in its history, and one which was not to be equalled until the twentieth century and its ordeal by fire in the Second World War.

(Overleaf) *Panorama of London circa 1616 by C. J. Visscher showing London Bridge. A typical street scene in front of the south gate house in what is now Borough High Street. Note the felons' heads on poles over the gate.*

23

St.Laurence Poultney

the Dutch Churche.

the Exchange.

St.Michaels

St.Peters.

Leadnle hall

Olde Swann

Fishmongers hall

THE BRIDGE

UVIUS

South

Warke

Winchester house

St. Mary Ouerts

St. Hellen

St. Andrew

St. Dunston in the east

Alhallowes Berking

Hackney

Custome

Lion Key

Billinsgate

Bridge gate

King Charles II (1660–1685) after Lely.

LONDON UNDER CHARLES II

Charles II, after his years in exile on the Continent, was restored in 1660, and the Londoners who had supported Parliament against his father went wild with relief. They were famished for gaiety, colour and laughter, and tired of the austerity of the Commonwealth when the arts had been held in check, and all imagination, to say nothing of luxury in dress and in the decoration of houses, had been looked upon as belonging to the Devil, and grass had grown between the paving-stones of deserted Whitehall. They had a king once more, and colour had come back into their lives. The day Charles entered his capital was also his birthday and this was a cause for a double celebration. John Evelyn made a note of this in his diary on 29 May 1660: 'He came with a triumph of over twenty thousand horse and foot brandishing their swords and shouting with unexpressible joy. The ways were strewn with flowers, the bells were ringing, the streets were hung with tapestry, and the fountains were running wine. The Mayor, Aldermen, and all the Companies, in their chains of gold, liveries and banners, were present; also, the lords and nobles. Everybody was clad in cloth of silver, gold and velvet; the windows and balconies were all set with ladies, trumpets and music, and myriads of people flocked the streets.'

The diarist, John Evelyn (1620–1706), from an engraving by R. Nanteuil.

Flying from the Plague, 1665, from a Broadside, 'London sounds the Trumpet'. Death rides with the rich who are able to escape to the country, but carry the plague with them.

The houses were hung with tapestry, the windows and balconies filled with ladies and the fountain flowed with wine again eleven months later for the King's coronation. He rode with 'a magnificent train on horseback, as rich as embroidery, velvet, cloth of gold, silk and jewels could make them and their prancing horses, proceeded through streets strewn with flowers. . . .'

THE PLAGUE

But, almost before the bells had stopped ringing, the first great disaster fell upon them: this was the Great Plague, and it began in the summer of 1665. It had come to London several times before in the sixteenth century. In 1563 Queen Elizabeth had ordered a gallows to be set up on the outskirts of Windsor to hang anybody hardy or foolish enough to try to escape from London, thereby bringing the infection with him to Windsor where the Court was taking refuge. It came again in 1604, the year following the death of the old Queen, and the first year of James's reign. Again the King and Court left London, and so it was in 1665. If you were fortunate enough to have the smallest of jobs about the Court you stood a much better chance of escaping the plague than most other people in London.

Laws passed in Elizabeth's reign and those of the first two Stuart kings, as well as during the Commonwealth, prohibited further house-building except on existing sites, and this resulted in terrible overcrowding in the houses of the poor. Yet more and more people poured into London, enticed by visions of getting rich quickly, or at least earning enough to provide them with some form of meal once a day. There was overcrowding in the City itself, as well as in Tower Hamlets on the further side of its eastern walls and the densely-packed area on the fringe of Westminster.

Records of population were not carefully kept during the seventeenth century in London, but the total figure for the city's inhabitants seems to vary between four and five hundred thousand. The people flocking into London usually found work either in the small workshops which thrived in the City, or they went 'into service' in the households of the wealthier citizens. When they did not find work, they frequently disappeared into the teeming warren of tiny streets in 'Alsatia', the thieves' kitchen in the area between what is now Fleet Street and the Thames, on the site of the old monastery of the White Friars. In medieval times this had been 'sanctuary' ground because it belonged to the Church, and anyone fleeing there was given shelter and immunity. Even after the dissolution of the monasteries by Henry VIII, the idea of sanctuary still held but, unfortunately, it applied to anyone seeking it, and that meant both the guilty and the innocent. All the thieves and cut-throats in London flocked to Alsatia and were lost in the fleabitten lodging-houses which lined its filthy alleyways. It was a kingdom of criminals, beggars and vagabonds who joined together in a kind of unholy brotherhood when they were faced with any attempt on the part of the aldermen or their constables to bring one of their fraternity to justice.

But there was overcrowding in other streets besides those of Alsatia, and this led to an even greater filth and stench. Trenches were dug out along the middle of most of the main thoroughfares, and into these was thrown all the refuse of the houses (usually hurled from the windows), human and animal excrement, garbage and offal from shops and markets, and the dead cats and dogs of the neighbourhood. When the smell grew beyond endurance, carts carried the refuse to special dumps in Grays Inn Road, Clerkenwell and Dowgate near London Bridge, all just beyond the city walls, and there it lay unattended. To our twentieth century noses, the smell would have been unbelievable. The wealthier people carried nosegays of herbs and sweet-smelling flowers when they walked abroad to counteract the effect of the noxious fumes rising from the streets: judges always carried them to provide an antidote to the smell of the wrongdoers brought before them. Nosegays are still carried today by the judge on the first two days of a new term in the High Court – purely as an interesting old custom! Most of the inhabitants of Alsatia would never have had a bath in their lives: even the average tradesman or master craftsman probably had only one bath a year. His heavy clothes – this was before the days of cheap cottons and light woollen manufacture – would get dirty and mudstained when it rained, in spite of the high pattens most people wore to lift them out of the mud. The streets were generally cobbled, sometimes not even that, and the rain turned them into quagmires.

Nevertheless, London was as healthy as any town in the known world at that time. It was refreshed by the winds blowing up from the Thames estuary with the changes of the tide. Still vaguely crescent-shaped, the City was less than half a mile wide at its broadest part and was surrounded by fields and heath on all sides. And there was plenty of rain to wash the streets.

But the rain was not enough: the dirt bred disease, especially in the hot weather, and it was a long, hot summer in 1665. The plague began about May, in the area of St Giles in the Fields, and crept on to St Andrew's, Holborn, to St Clement Dane's, St Martin's in the Fields and then reached Westminster. It took just under six months to travel from the western to the eastern suburbs of the City. In May, the death toll was estimated to be somewhere in the region of 31000. The total number of deaths was about one-fifth of the population of London, so far as can be estimated – that is, around one hundred thousand, taking

The Great Plague 1666 – the death-cart: 'Bring out your dead!', the handbell and the cross on the door of a plague-stricken house.

into account the number of deaths from the 'spotted fever' which was also prevalent. Many people registered the deaths in their families as occurring from the spotted fever in order to escape the restrictions imposed by the Lord Mayor and Aldermen to contain the pestilence.

'Orders conceived and published . . . concerning the Infection of the Plague' was the title of the small book printed by the Lord Mayor and Aldermen. Directions were given in it for the appointment of a number of 'Examiners' who would keep themselves informed and up-to-date on the state of the plague in their parish. Any house that was known to contain someone ill with the plague was immediately shut up, bolted and barred – nailed up if need be – and no one was allowed to enter except authorised persons such as doctors, 'nurse-keepers' or 'searchers', who were respectable women employed to inspect the bodies after death and determine whether their death had been caused by the plague or any other illness, such as the spotted fever. Only the doctors or nurse-keepers were allowed to fetch food or medicine, and when they left a plague-stricken house they took the keys with them.

At night, carts were driven through the streets. All the doors of the plague-stricken houses were marked with a large red cross with the words 'Lord have mercy on us' above it. The drivers of the carts called out 'Bring out your dead!', and the bodies were carried away to large communal graveyards to be buried in quicklime. Two burial grounds were in the east, both lying off the river – one near what is now the opening to the Regent's Canal, and the other on the Isle of Dogs.

A deep and ominous silence lay over the City which was in truth a city of the dead. There were no busy throngs of people passing by in the streets, no hawkers' cries, no coaches and no hooves clattering over the cobblestones. Everyone who could afford to do so had left the City, and only a few conscientious officials, such as the other famous diarist, and perhaps the greatest, Samuel Pepys. He was employed as Clerk of the Acts to the Navy, and he lived in Seething Lane in the parish of St Olave, by the Minories and the Tower. On 20 September, 1665 he wrote in his diary: 'To Lambeth. But, Lord! what a sad time it is to see no boats upon the River; and grass grows all up and down Whitehall court, and nobody but poor wretches in the streets!'

Modern medical science has been able to identify the Great Plague as the bubonic plague. This is carried by a particular kind of flea which, unlike most parasites living off animals, also lives off humans. Rats infested the streets and came into the houses – even the most well-kept house was likely to have mice and a rat or two – and the fleas transferred themselves from the rats to the inhabitants of the house.

The (Bubonic) Plague was carried by a flea living as a parasite on the black rat.

In the year after the Plague it had been another long, hot summer and the densely-packed houses in the area around the foot of London Bridge on the north bank creaked with dryness. The laws prohibiting new building meant that many of the old houses which should have been knocked down and replaced in regular streets were not. They were patched up with the original materials of wood and plaster while their beams sagged and rotted. In a dry period they were kindling for any stray spark, and a fire would blaze in a matter of seconds. The Londoners were always conscious of this danger, and the fires were usually brought under control without too much delay. Most streets could provide a number of large hooks for pulling down the thatch from the roofs in order to prevent the fire from spreading.

In the early hours of Sunday 2 September 1666, the King's baker, Thomas Farynor, or Farriner, and his daughter were woken by clouds of smoke to find their house and bakery on fire. They climbed on to the roof of their house in Pudding Lane and were eventually rescued. The fire could have been started by one of the ovens not being sufficiently damped down, so that a spark could have set the kindling alight. Various unfortunate foreigners – for the Londoner was as anti-foreigner as he had ever been – were hauled before the magistrates charged with beginning the fire and, in the end, the son of a French watchmaker confessed to the crime. No one knew exactly why he did this, because the Farynors themselves were able to prove that he had not entered their house. But a victim was needed to assuage the anger of the citizens and, as he was willing, he was hanged.

Streets, such as Fish Street Hill, leading down to the river, contained warehouses which were filled with inflammable goods including tar, hemp, oils and spirits. An east wind blew sparks into a neighbouring inn-yard where it caught the straw in the stables. Then the fire whipped through Thames Street, which was full of warehouses, devoured the church of St Magnus the Martyr at the foot of London Bridge, and swept along the Bridge itself, destroying about a third of the houses on the northern half. Fire was raging along all the river wharves.

The Lord Mayor at first underestimated the force of the flames, and thought that the citizens could contain it by organizing chains of men passing along leather buckets of water. He soon had to admit that he was wrong. The fire turned inwards from the river towards the City itself: All Hallows the Less and All Hallows the Great were the first of the churches to be totally destroyed. People began to collect their

Leather bucket and helmet used by firemen after the Great Fire of 1666.

belongings together and swarm out of town, using what transport they could lay their hands on.

This time the King stayed in London, and Pepys, who worked closely in Naval affairs with the King's brother, the Duke of York, hurried to tell him of conditions prevailing on the first day of the Fire: 'Having staid, and in an hour's time seen the fire rage in every way, and nobody to my sight endeavouring to quench it, but to remove their goods, and leave all to the fire, and having seen it get as far as the Steele-yard and the wind mighty high and driving it into the City: and every thing after so long a drought proving combustible, even the very stones of churches. . . . I to White Hall (with a gentleman with me, who desired to go off from the Tower, to see the fire, in my boat): and there up to the King's closet in the Chapel where people come about me and I did give them an account dismayed them all, and word was carried in to the King. So I was called for, and did tell the King and Duke of York what I saw and that unless his Majesty did command houses to be pulled down, nothing could stop the fire. They seemed much troubled, and the King commanded me to go to my Lord Mayor from him, and command him to spare no houses, but to pull down before the fire every way. . . .'

Pepys went with his wife and some friends in a boat on the river to survey the scene. The Thames was crammed with lighters and small boats transporting people's household goods to the South Bank, and the ever-observant Pepys noted that nearly one boat in three was

carrying a pair of virginals among these goods, which says much for the musical nature of the Londoners at this time. The wind changed and drove the smoke over the river and into their faces so they disembarked near 'a little ale-house on the Bankside, over against the Three Cranes, and there staid until it was dark almost, and saw the fire grow, and as it grew darker, appeared more and more, and in corners and upon steeples, and between churches and houses, so that we could see up the hill of the City, in a most horrid malicious bloody flame, not like the fine flame of an ordinary fire. . . . We staid till, it being darkish, we saw the fire as only one entire arch of fire from this to the other side the bridge, and in a bow up the hill for an arch of above a mile long; it made me weep to see it. The churches, houses, and all on fire, and flaming at once; and a horrid noise the flames made, and the cracking of houses in their ruine. . . .' He also noted that the pigeons found it difficult to fly because their wings were singed by the flames.

In the beginning, the people were so astounded that the fire got a strong hold before they brought themselves round to doing anything about it. Evelyn said that 'There was nothing heard or seen but crying out and lamentation, and running about like distracted creatures without at all attempting to save even their goods.' The pavements glowed red with the heat, and neither man nor horse was able to tread the cobbles. The King personally supervised the organization, and gave orders for buildings to be blown up by gunpowder by his seamen who were on shore at that time: this did not make him very popular with some aldermen and powerful tradesmen whose houses stood in the way. But the open spaces between the houses did help to contain the fire a little. Charles and the Duke of York moved among their people, physically joining in the fire-fighting at times, and encouraging the citizens to do all in their power to save what they could of the City. A little later the King took his barge on the river and surveyed the tearing, roaring curtain of flame that enveloped everything in its path. St Paul's Cathedral, the Royal Exchange, the houses and shops in Cornhill, Cannon Street, Eastcheap, Gracechurch Street and the Companies' Hall were completely destroyed. On 7 September John Evelyn recorded a walk through the City: 'It was only with extraordinary difficulty – clambering over mountains of yet smoking rubbish and frequently mistaking where I was, the ground under my feet being so hot that it made me not only sweat but even burnt the soles of my shoes. I was infinitely concerned to find that goodly church, St Paul's, a sad ruin and that beautiful portico – for structure comparable to any in Europe, and not long before repaired by the late King – now rent in pieces.' The portico to which Evelyn referred was the one built by Inigo Jones when Charles I set about restoring the Cathedral. The stonework split and the lead on the roof melted, as well as all the beautiful gold plate ornaments of the altar. To Evelyn's sorrow, 'The exquisitely wrought Mercers' Chapel, the sumptuous Exchange, the august fabric of Christchurch, the Companies' Halls, sumptuous buildings, arches and entries all lay in dust. The fountains were dried up and ruined, whilst the very waters remained boiling.' The water standard in Cornhill had somehow remained undamaged, and the effigy of Queen Elizabeth on Ludgate was untouched, later to be placed on the front of St Dunstan's in the West where it can be seen today. The hinges, bars and gates of the lock-ups and gatehouse prisons were melted, and many a malefactor had reason to bless the fire that set him free. The narrow streets were choked with rubble and rubbish, and it was only possible to walk through the broader ones. Even so, Evelyn found the heat so intense that his hair was almost singed and his feet were 'insufferably sore'. It was only possible to tell where one was by the bell-tower or the steeple of some church sticking out of the ruins.

He went towards Islington and Highgate 'where one might have

Even the rise of modern office blocks cannot dwarf the splendour of Wren's masterpiece; St Paul's Cathedral as it is today.

seen two hundred thousand people, of all ranks and degrees, dispersed and lying alongside their heaps of what they could save from the *Incendium*, deploring their loss, and yet, though ready to perish for hunger and destitution, not asking one penny for relief – which to me appeared a stranger sight than any I had yet beheld. His Majesty and Council indeed took all imaginable care for their relief, by proclamation for the country people to come in and refresh them with provisions'.

The fire raged for four days and had almost petered out by the early hours of Thursday morning. Thousands of people were rendered homeless, over 13000 houses were destroyed, forty-four City Companies' halls and eighty-seven churches. Only ten churches were left standing. The City has seen nothing comparable with this devastation until the early autumn days of 1940. Five-sixths of the City had been laid waste and, when the Londoners returned home, a shanty town mushroomed on the empty foundations of what had once been the proudest capital in Europe.

Pepys and Evelyn knew one another reasonably well, and shared a mutual respect; they were also both members of the Royal Society which Charles had instituted in the second year of his reign for the furtherance of knowledge in all fields. Pepys reported Evelyn saying to him that 'none of the nobility had come out of the country at all to help the King, or comfort him or prevent commotions at this fire; but do as if the King were nobody; nor e'er a priest comes to give the King and Court good council, or to comfort the poor people that suffer; but all is dead, nothing of good in any of their minds. . . .'

Rich and poor alike suffered in the fire, but whereas the wealthy man was able to transport his money, plate and goods to the country where he often had another house, the tradesman returned to find his shop or workshop in ruins, his tools melted into lumps of metal, and his stock vanished. The Londoners, understandably, seemed to be sinking beneath the load of their double disaster and to be fearful of yet another catastrophe approaching. There was much superstitious talk of comets and prophecies, and many were sure that all their troubles were to be laid at the door of France.

Pepys gave his own view of the Londoner's state of mind in his entry for 7 September 1666, six days after the outbreak of the Great Fire: '. . . by water to Paul's Wharfe. Walked thence, and saw all the towne burned, and a miserable sight of Paul's church, with all the roofe fallen, and the body of the quire fallen into St Fayth's [a separate church in the crypt under the choir of old St Paul's]. Paul's school also, Ludgate and Fleet-street. My father's house, and the church, and a good part of the

Temple the like . . . To Sir W. Coventry, at St James, who lay without curtains, having removed all his goods; as the King at White Hall, and every body had done, and was doing. He hopes we shall have no public distractions upon this fire, which is what every body fears, because of the talk of the French having a hand in it. And it is a proper time for discontents; but all men's minds are full of care to protect themselves, and save their goods; the militia is in arms everywhere.'

But the citizens of London were never going to be caught so unprepared again. After the fire, the City was divided into four parts. Each part was to provide 800 buckets, fifty ladders, two brass hand-syringes, twenty-four pickaxe sledges and forty large shovels. Each of the twelve great City Companies had a fire-engine, thirty buckets, three ladders, six pickaxe sledges and two hand-syringes. And each Company had to appoint two masters, four journeymen, eight apprentices and sixteen labourers to be ready to respond to any alarum of fire.

John Lofting's Fire Engine, being tried out apparently in front of the New Exchange. King Charles II gave it his approval. Note the boy in the foreground whose job seems to be straightening out the hose. Engraving by J. Kip in London Prospect's Portfolio.

3
Rebuilding the City

CHARLES II was anxious that his capital should be rebuilt in as beautiful and durable a style as possible, but he also realized that people needed shelter quickly, and that something had to be done to bring back the rich men and merchants who had fled to their country houses in Knightsbridge and Kensington in the west and Islington and Hampstead in the north. So he issued a proclamation on 13 September stating that any new buildings must be made from brick and stone, and that streets should be made wide enough to allow for the passage of traffic and pedestrians, varying in width with the importance of the street. All claims to land held before the Fire were to be respected, providing that the owners built upon them in accordance with the plans to be issued by the six Commissioners for the Rebuilding of London. Three of these Commissioners were selected by the King, the other three by the City. John Evelyn was not slow in presenting his plan – a very good one – for the rebuilding, for he recorded in his diary for September of that year: 'On the 10th I went again to the ruins, for it was now no longer a city. On the 13th, I presented His Majesty with a survey of the ruins and a plan for a new city.' It seems probable that he had realized some time before the fire the need for improvement.

The best known of the Commissioners – one of the King's men – was

Sir Christopher Wren (1632–1723). The architect of St Paul's Cathedral, the Royal Hospital, Chelsea, Greenwich Hospital and a number of London churches. Portrait by J. B. Closterman.

a young professor of astronomy, interested in many things, who was also an extremely gifted architect: Dr, later Sir, Christopher Wren. He said that everything should be knocked down in the City and a new beginning made. He wanted a great deal of open spaces or piazzas, with wide streets, and a new St Paul's Cathedral and a new Royal Exchange as the principal focal points: all the streets would radiate from them. In common with Evelyn, Wren wanted to make all the dirty wharves from Blackfriars to Billingsgate into a wide paved walk lined with gracious houses and public buildings, which would have given London's shabby, busy waterfront a rare beauty and a completely new look.

FINANCING THE WORK

But there was not time to wait for all these improvements: the homeless needed shelter straight away and business had to be set in motion again. Furthermore, there was very little money. The City was very poor: the plague had left thousands of orphans, some of which were cared for by the various parishes. The Fire had destroyed all wealth, and the State coffers had been almost emptied by the costly and calamitous war with Holland. And there were differences between the Commissioners and the people who owned the land, while shopkeepers and merchants were demanding compensation.

Money had always been a matter for disagreement between the Stuart kings and the City of London. James I had borrowed from the City when it had been in a flourishing condition, and it had managed to assimilate this but, when his son, Charles I, levied 'Tonnage and Poundage' taxes on imports into the Pool of London in 1629, the City rose in outrage and, because the merchants refused to carry on business while the taxes were imposed, there was hardly any trade for several months. The 'Ship Money' levy was one of the various reasons for the outbreak of the Civil War. Cromwell borrowed from the City too and, in 1652, it gave him over £1000 for the war against the Dutch. Upon the Declaration of Charles II as King on 1 May 1660, Parliament borrowed £100000 from the City: half of it was sent to the Hague to Charles who, almost penniless, was waiting to embark for his kingdom, and the other half was used by Parliament in various ways, not least of which was Charles's splendid coronation. The City Companies raised £10000 for Charles on their own initiative and £2000 to be divided between his brothers, the Dukes of York and Gloucester. The borrowings went on all through Charles's reign and, in 1671, he took the extremely rash step of closing the Exchequer – rash because it antagonized the City in no uncertain fashion. It meant that the King would make no repayments nor pay interest on a loan to the amount of six million pounds sterling.

In the same year 1671, such was the mixture of the practical and impractical which made up this strange, intelligent, cynical, extravagant man who was king, Charles passed an act through Parliament which was to have a far-reaching effect on London's own government. This was for the 'better Paving and Cleansing of the Streets and Sewers in and about the City of London'. To carry this out, the Common Council of London appointed representatives of the whole City area to form a body of Commissioners of Sewers. The idea was a good and most necessary one, for London's streets were as filthy as they had been in Tudor times, but nothing very much was accomplished. But the important thing was that, for the first time, London was considered as a whole area. Previously, all work and improvements had been carried out by each parish of the City separately; now they were all fused into one corporation for the purpose of the act. This was the very beginning of the Greater London we know today.

When the question of who was going to pay for the rebuilding of London arose, Charles answered it to some extent by imposing, through Parliament, a tax on all coal imports into the Port of London to help pay for the immediate rebuilding, for compensation and for the building of the new St Paul's and the City churches, as well as the Monument which was to remind generations to come of the greatest disaster in London's history. The coal tax was not popular because Cromwell had allowed 400 chauldrons [a chauldron or chaldron equalled thirty-six bushels] to be imported free of tax into London every year for the poor.

THE PLANS

Although the various plans put forward by the Commissioners and other responsible people had to be shelved, some good things were done. Rules were made regarding the type of house to be built and the materials to be used for it. There were to be no more overhanging storeys – all the fronts of the houses were to be flat. In important streets the houses were to be four storeys high, in less important ones they were to be three storeys or less. However, the shelving of the plans for the complete rebuilding of the City meant that London had lost its last chance of becoming a *planned* city instead of an urban sprawl, and we are still paying the cost of that lost city today.

One of Wren's plans was realized. The Fleet Canal or the Ditch, as it was more commonly known, had for centuries been an eyesore and a gross offence to the nose. Every kind of refuse and ordure was thrown into this stream which flowed from the north through Holborn southwards to the river. Its course today, so far as we can trace it above ground, would flow down Farringdon Street, under Holborn Viaduct Bridge and out into the Thames at Blackfriars. Wren's first care was to rid the City of London of this loathsome sore which lay on its western boundary, and he had the Ditch cleaned out and unsilted. It was 1674 before the fifty foot canal was made navigable for river traffic again. But, alas, no one seemed to want to use it, and it became something of a white elephant. Gradually, it silted up again and became London's principal dustbin once more. Later on, in 1766, a hundred years after the Fire, it was filled in and became an underground sewer.

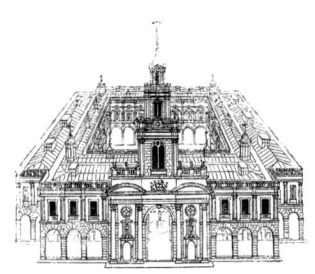

The New Exchange, or Britain's Burse in the Strand, opened by James I in 1608. Design for front elevation.

CHURCHES

The Guildhall and the Royal Exchange were rebuilt within a few years after the Fire and, within a decade, Sir Christopher Wren had taken in

The courtyard of the Royal Exchange rebuilt after the Great Fire of 1666.

hand at least half of the fifty-one churches he was to rebuild. Among the Wren churches were St Mary Aldermary and St Andrew-by-the-Wardrobe both in what is now called Queen Victoria Street, St Clement in Eastcheap, St Edmund King and Martyr in Lombard Street; St Benet down by the river on Paul's Wharf (the church where Inigo Jones was buried), the famous St Mary-le-Bow, the church of 'Bow Bells', and St Lawrence Jewry by the Guildhall which was, and still is, the Corporation church of the City of London. All these churches and others by Sir Christopher Wren still stand, although nearly all of them were damaged in the bombing during the Second World War and have since been repaired. They rank amongst the greatest works of man to be found in our country and, as such, are the subject of pilgrimages by people from all over the world.

SIR CHRISTOPHER WREN

As Inigo Jones had come under the Italian influence, so Christopher Wren reflected the influence of France. He had been in Paris in 1665, aged twenty-three, when the palace of the Louvre had been under construction and had met artists and architects, such as the great Bernini and Mansard, who were attached to the court of Louis XIV. He did not only confine his studies to Paris, but visited the Renaissance

42

buildings in the surrounding countryside. The French ideas he imbibed coincided with those of Charles II who had spent much time in France and admired most things French. He built much in white Portland stone which has very good weathering properties, although during the reign of William III, who came from the Netherlands, and his consort, Mary, Wren built also in red brick with a strong Dutch influence. This can also be seen in the building he carried out at Hampton Court for William and Mary, and in the mixture of brick and stone he used for the rebuilding of St Benet's. When Charles commissioned him to carry out the building of Greenwich Palace, however, it was in the French style. He worked in many styles, but always in the one which was most suited to the local background and climate. Besides the palaces, he carried out designs for houses for the wealthier citizens to live in. In the design of his churches he always gave pre-eminence to the altar, font and pulpit which are, after all, the most important parts of a church. Sometimes his churches are built in the form of a cross, sometimes they are domed, sometimes with a wide side aisle in the main body of the church. All have clear glass to give full value to the paintings in the church, particularly behind the altar, and to the richness of the wood carving.

GRINLING GIBBONS

Greenwich Hospital, now the Royal Naval College, begun in 1696 by Sir Christopher Wren. The building took nearly 30 years to complete and is the combined work of three of our greatest architects: Wren, Hawksmoor and Vanburgh.

John Evelyn had introduced Wren, and his other friend Samuel Pepys, to 'that incomparable young man' Grinling Gibbons, the greatest carver Britain has known. He had discovered him in an isolated cottage not far from his country estate, Sayes Court, near Deptford, where he was copying in wood Tintoretto's picture of the Crucifixion, which Evelyn had seen in Venice. He coaxed the young woodcarver to

London and introduced him in March 1671 to the King who was also to be a great admirer of his genius. Evelyn had hoped that the King would buy the carving of the Crucifixion and, indeed, he seemed to be on the point of doing so when he was called away and left the Queen to carry on with the business. However, she was influenced by a 'French peddling woman', as Evelyn called her, a Madame de Bordes, against the work, greatly to Evelyn's anger. But Christopher Wren 'faithfully promised me to employ him for the future', and in fact did so, as we can see from the beautiful pulpit and font in St James's, Piccadilly. Unfortunately, not much of Gibbons's work remains to us today, but a wonderful example of his skill may be seen in the 'lace' cravat carved in a light-coloured wood which is in the Victoria and Albert Museum.

An extraordinary example of the woodcarver's art: a man's cravat carved in limewood to resemble linen and guipure lace by Grinling Gibbons (1648–1720).

ST PAUL'S CATHEDRAL

Without a doubt, Wren's greatest achievement was the building of the new St Paul's Cathedral. Inigo Jones had never been able, through lack of money chiefly, to complete the work he had begun with the west front. The interior, until the Fire, was dirty and still used as a public meeting-place and employment exchange as it had been in Elizabethan times. Fruit and vegetables were still carted through the sacred precincts from one side to the other, as they had been for the past

century or so. In fact the Cathedral, badly in need of repair, ought to have been pulled down before it was burned down in 1666.

Wren submitted his plans on the 11 September; the fire had only abated on the 7th. Like Evelyn, he had lost no time. Charles gave the royal warrant for proceeding with the work in May 1675, but it was not completed until thirty-five years later. Wren would not build on the old foundations, as he considered them too unsound, and an accident to a workman confirmed this. He also took the then novel course of employing a battering-ram and gunpowder, very precisely calculated, for the purposes of demolition. After many re-drafts of his original plan he based the main feature of the Cathedral on the great dome of St Peter's in Rome by Bramante.

In its construction, over fifty thousand tons of Portland stone were used, besides thousands of tons of rubble, timber and marble. Londoners had never seen anything like it before: the gold cross on the beautiful dome could be seen from afar glinting in the sun, and it became accepted as a symbol of London. Although two world wars in the twentieth century were to spread devastation all around the Cathedral, the cross still remained as a reminder to the Londoners that there was a spirit in their city which could not be defeated.

The idea of London rising from the ashes was expressed in Wren's first design for the Monument; this was a slender column decorated with tongues of flame up its stem; and a phoenix rising from flames at its summit. But the design accepted by the Royal Commission was a Doric column with a burst of gilded flames, without a phoenix, at the very top. It was placed at the bottom of Fish Street Hill, 202 feet in height, and situated 202 feet away from the site of the baker's shop in Pudding Lane where the Fire began. It contains 311 steps leading to the

The Monument, which is 202 feet high, and stands 202 feet from the house in Pudding Lane where the Great Fire began in 1666. Engraving circa 1680.

balcony at the top from where you could see London spread out in a panorama, when the smoke which rose from all the small industrial workshops in London did not obscure the view. Even before the Fire, Evelyn had presented a treatise to the King entitled *Fumifugium: or the inconvenience of the air and smoke of London dissipated*. The King was so pleased that he commanded Evelyn to print it, but it did not seem to make much difference to the smog of London. It is still possible to climb to the top of the Monument today, but it is no longer the highest building in London, and it is dwarfed by the high office buildings which surround it.

Sir Christopher Wren was a very old man when the Cathedral was finished in 1710, and his son completed the work by placing in position the final stone of the lantern. The greatest of English architects was not to die until 1723, and he was buried under the choir of his own Cathedral. On a tablet over the inner north doorway is his epitaph in Latin: 'Si monumentum requiris circumspice' – 'If you need a monument [for Wren,] look around you'.

4
The development of London

THE London of Charles II was no longer the one square mile of the City itself; it had begun to spread and to take on the earliest form of the Greater London we know today. The villages of Stephney and Whitechapel grew and expanded beyond the eastern walls, and Mile End marked the limit of one mile from the city wall. Hampstead and Islington in the north were still in the country, but were visited more and more for their healthy air which was such a relief after the heavily polluted air of coal-burning London. The villages of Deptford and Rotherhithe across the river began to expand as well, as this expansion of the capital continued, partly owing to the increased trade and partly to the people pouring in to the capital to find work in the many small industries, in the building trade and in the brickfields.

TRADE

In 1685, after King Louis XIV of France had withdrawn toleration of the Protestants, or Huguenots, a large number of French refugees settled in the Spitalfields area in the east of London. Many of these were skilled silk-weavers, and Spitalfields became famous for its manufacture of

47

1. St. Clements.
2. St. Dunstans.
3. St. Brides.
4. St. Andrews.
5. St. Sepulchers.
6. Little St. Bartholomews.
7. St. Martins Ludgate.
8. St. Andrews Warbroke.
9. Christs Church.
10. St. Bennet Paulswharf.
11. St. Pauls Cathedral.
12. St. Mary - Magdalen.
13. St. Austins.
14. St. Nicolas Coleabby.
15. St. Mary Somerset.
16. Alhallows Broadstreet.
17. St. Mildred Broadstreet.
18. St. Michael Queenstreet.
19. St. Marye Bow.
20. St. Mary Aldermary.
21. St. James Garlick Hill.
22. St. Laurence.
23. St. Antholins Watlinstreet.
24. St. Michael Royal.
25. Alhallows the Great.
26. St. Stephen Walbrook.
27. St. Margaret Lothbury.
28. St. Swithin.
29. The Royal Exchange.
30. St. Clements East cheap.
31. St. Michael Crooked Lane.
32. St. Mary Abchurch.
33. St. Michael Cornhill.
34. St. Peters Cornhill.
35. St. Thomas.

A PROSPECT

woven silk. Jewish refugees expelled from Amsterdam came to London, many again settling in the east where they were employed in the textile trades.

Trade and industry grew during the reigns of the Stuarts: London was the port for the reception of the greater part of overseas trade whether it was destined for north, south, east or west. Bristol and Norwich, the next largest cities and ports, contained about 30000 citizens each, whereas London numbered somewhere between four and five hundred thousand inhabitants.

DOCKS AND WHARVES

In spite of the increased import and export business of the capital, little was done after the Fire to build more wharves and docks to accommodate it. Three new quays were built in 1665, but they were insufficient to deal with the increase in trade which developed as the smaller ports in East Anglia, such as King's Lynn, declined for various

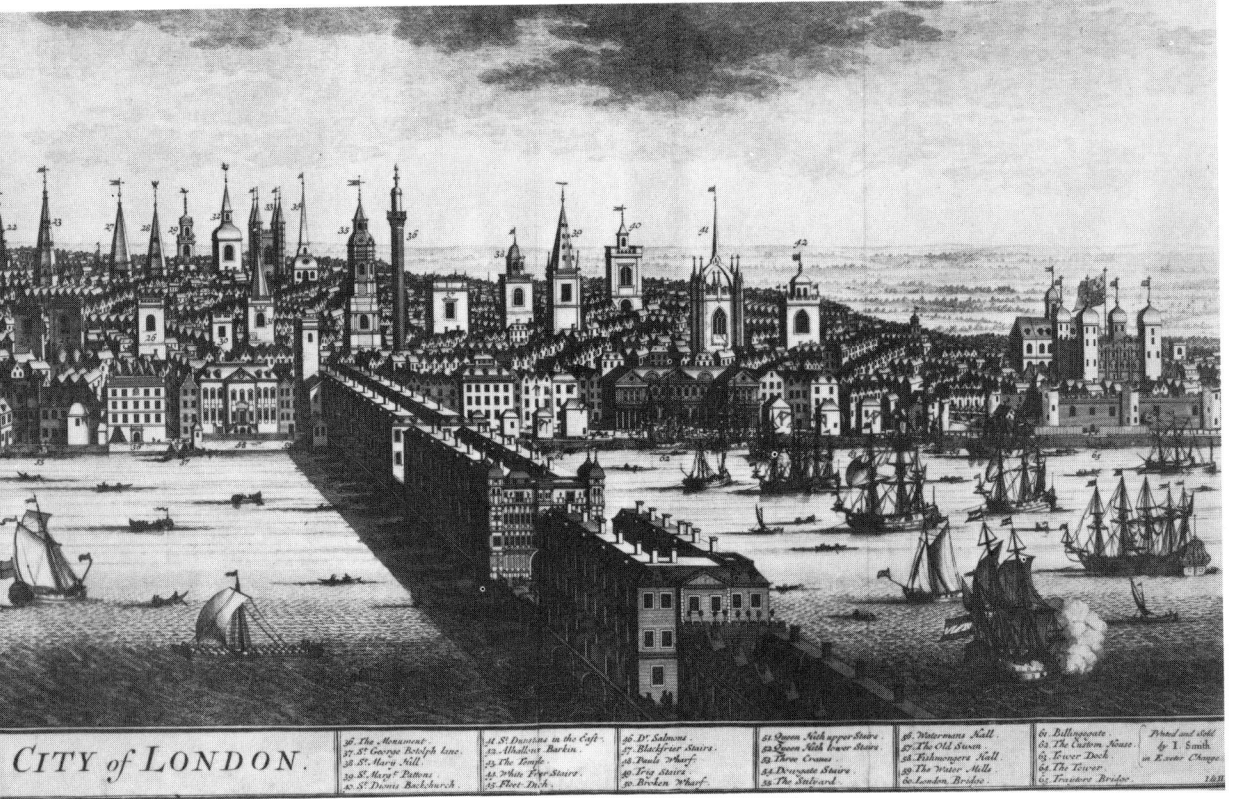

CITY of LONDON.

36 The Monument.	41 St Dunstans in the East.	46 Dr Salmons.	51 Queen Nith upper Stairs.	56 Watermans Hall.	61 Billingsgate.	Printed and Sold
37 St George Botolph lane.	42 Alhallows Barkin.	47 Blackfryer Stairs.	52 Queen Nith lower Stairs.	57 The Old Swan.	62 The Custom House.	by I. Smith
38 St Mary Hill.	43 The Temple.	48 Pauls Wharf.	53 Three Cranes.	58 Fishmongers Hall.	63 Tower Dock.	in Exeter Change.
39 St Mary Pattens.	44 White Fryer Stairs.	49 Trig Stairs.	54 Dowgate Stairs.	59 The Water Mills.	64 The Tower.	
40 St Dennis Backchurch.	45 Fleet Ditch.	50 Broken Wharf.	55 The Stilyard.	60 London Bridge.	65 Traators Bridge.	1611

reasons and the trade shifted to London. In 1661, Pepys recorded that he went to the East India Dock at Millwall where merchandise for the East India Company was unloaded. Another dock was built at Rotherhithe which was known first as Howland's Dock, then as Greenland Dock. Now it forms part of the Surrey Dock complex which has only recently fallen into disuse.

In 1669, Billingsgate, which had been a general wharf until then, was made a wharf only for fish, and it became a free wharf. Those ships which were not able to find a wharf to take their goods had to unload their cargoes into small boats or 'lighters' which were then rowed to shore by lightermen.

THE POOL OF LONDON

It is hard for us to imagine what the Pool of London from the Bridge to the Tower must have looked like. All sizes and nationalities of ships were to be found there, making a forest of masts and spars, with usually

only a few feet of water between one vessel and the next. Large ships under sail from the Lowlands or Scandinavia would jostle against dirty little colliers bringing coal from Newcastle to feed the greedy jaws of London's industries, while skiffs and wherries carrying passengers, ferrying from one bank to the other, would narrowly but skilfully miss the royal yacht as the watermen energetically plied their oars.

The river was still a highway for London, whether for the King to make a progress in his heavily gilded and ornately painted barge, or for someone such as Pepys who took an afternoon off to go 'to Southwark-fair, very dirty, and there was the puppet-show of Whittington, which was pretty to see; and how that idle thing do work upon people that see it, and even myself too! And thence to Jacob Hall's dancing on the ropes, where I saw such action as I never saw before, and mightily worth seeing. . . .' It was still easier to go by boat than to ride or take a coach, provided you disembarked before coming to the Bridge and walked to its other side, there to embark again, for the currents were still as rapid through the Bridge, and as dangerous, as they had been in earlier centuries.

The busy Port of London as Pepys would probably have recognized it.

The old eleventh-century bridge still stood over the river, with shops and dwelling-houses on either of a central roadway no broader than twelve feet in places. About one-third of the shops and houses at the northern end of the Bridge had been damaged in the Fire and had been replaced, but the old gabled houses almost met overhead in the middle of the roadway and projected over the river itself. The Bridge was probably the scene of London's first traffic-jam because the traffic had often been brought to a standstill in Tudor days; but now that carriages were increasing in number and were no longer a royal or aristocratic prerogative, the congestion became far worse.

In 1634, the first sedan-chair was used, most probably by the Duke of Buckingham and, in the same year, four hackney-coaches were put on public hire by a Captain Bailey who obviously knew a good thing when he saw it. The hackney-coach had first been seen towards the end of Elizabeth's reign, old John Stow wrote in his Survey: 'the world runs in wheels with many whose parents were glad to goe on foot'. Cromwell limited the number of hackney-coaches in London to two hundred and these had to be licensed by the Mayor and the Corporation.

With so much traffic, clatter of wheels on cobbles and danger to life and limb on the Bridge, many people were content to use the ferries, although they had the inconvenience of disembarking and re-embarking. But road transport was beginning to get a hold, and no one

A sedan-chair which was in general use in London streets by 1649.

resented this more than the many thousands of watermen who earned their living by rowing their wherries to and fro and up and down the Thames. The wherry was a small boat with six or eight oars and a covering for the heads of the passengers. The watermen used to stand at the top of the river stairs calling out 'Oars! Oars!'. One celebrated waterman, John Taylor, was also a would-be poet, and he churned out hundreds of doggerel verses about the joys and tribulations of being a waterman. He came from Gloucestershire, but settled in London as a young man, living the hard life of a waterman, using their private language and often sleeping in his boat to prevent it, being stolen. The watermen seem to have been colourful personalities and delighted in slanging-matches between themselves when they came up close to one another. From many points of view, they appear to have had something in common with the modern London taxi-driver. Taylor was recognized as a leading light among his brethren, and devoted much of his poetry to invective against coaches and those who rode in them. But he was known outside his own river-world too, because he organized a water pageant in 1613 in honour of James I's daughter, Elizabeth, on the occasion of her betrothal to the Prince Palatine. After the Restoration, when the theatres which had been closed down in Cromwell's time were re-opened, many were on the north bank, and this meant a considerable drop in the watermen's earnings as they were no longer needed to ferry theatre-goers over to Southwark.

CITY WALLS

The ancient city walls still stood at the beginning of the century and, in the eastern and western parts which had escaped the Fire, some of the old houses could still be seen – in Crutched Friars, Cripplegate and West Smithfield. Even a few of the old monastic ruins had escaped, and these were thought to be very old indeed in 1660; such buildings were St Katherine's by the Tower, the Charterhouse, St Bartholomew's the Great, and the Tudor gateway which had belonged to the Priory of the Knights Hospitallers of the Order of St John. Gradually, as the century progressed, the walls of the City were not maintained and crumbled into disrepair. The gates of the City lasted until the middle of the eighteenth century.

In the freezing winter of 1698 a careless maid set White Hall Palace on fire. She worked for one of the officials of the Palace, and had left her master's clothes to dry too near a fire. The clothes were soon alight and, before long, the whole Palace went up in flames. All that remained were the Banqueting House, which exists today, and two gateways which have since disappeared. After that, the royal couple, William and Mary, made their home in Kensington Palace. It was a pity because, apart from the churches, it was one of the few remaining buildings of Tudor London left standing after the Fire, and James II, who succeeded his brother Charles II for only three years before he was deposed in the 'Glorious Revolution' of 1688, had spent quite a lot of money in redecorating it.

One of the greatest changes in the appearance of London was the development of streets of houses and of squares. This development was not in the City itself, but to its west and north, outside the walls, and there was a great deal of money involved.

During Cromwell's time, those nobles who were not Parliamentarians had kept the peace for the most part and bided their time: they had lived quietly on their country estates with as little outward display as possible. Any ostentation or deliberate show of wealth would have brought disapproval and possible removal of that wealth by the more severe element of the Puritans.

THE RESTORATION

But with the Restoration of Charles II there was a return to the old atmosphere of luxury and delight in the material comforts that riches brought. There was also a great deal of heedless extravagance and licentiousness. The King, after years of poverty when a young man in exile in Europe, seemed to be making up for lost time: not for nothing was he known as the Merry Monarch. He was an intelligent man and a cynical one, but he was also capable of gestures of compassion and generosity to individuals, and he remembered those who had been with him in the bad times. One such was Henry St Jermyn; Earl of St Albans, who was in many ways an unscrupulous man, but at times he had been of help to Charles and to his mother, the Dowager Queen, Henrietta Maria.

There had been no building inside or outside the walls, other than

Queen Henrietta Maria married Charles I in 1625 and lived to see her son, Charles, restored to the throne of England. Detail of a portrait by an unknown artist.

rebuilding on old sites as houses were burned, or fell down, since Inigo Jones's piazza in Covent Garden. But some of the nobility returning to London saw that it was ready for redevelopment and, since they owned or could buy parcels of land outside the city walls, asked Charles for permission to build. In most cases, either because he was grateful to them for one reason or another, or because they might be useful to him, he gave permission.

ST JAMES'S FIELDS

Charles had always liked St James's Fields to the south of the Palace and, soon after his return from exile, he had had it re-stocked with trees to replace those chopped down for fuel by the Puritans. He made a lake and put ducks on it because he liked to feed them, stocked it with deer and laid down gravel paths so that he could take those long, quick walks, preferably accompanied by dogs, that all the Stuart kings liked so much. He also laid out an 'alley' for the playing of a game rather like croquet. This was called *pêle-mêle* in France, where Charles had learned to play it, or *palla a maglio*, meaning 'ball to mallet' in its original Italian.

Pall Mall, as it is called today, was the border of the south side of St James's Field; on the north the boundary was the road to Knightsbridge which we now know as Piccadilly. The eastern boundary was the Haymarket and the western St James's Street leading from the Palace.

Henry Jermyn asked the King for the lease of half of St James's Fields, and later obtained its freehold. Still later, he asked for and received a lease on the rest of the Field. He then began to build terraces of houses in streets still known as King Street, Jermyn Street and Duke Street, with St James's Square as the centrepiece.

He commissioned Sir Christopher Wren to build the church, and Wren produced what he considered to be one of his finest buildings: St James's, Piccadilly. This was consecrated in 1685. Here are to be found two of the loveliest pieces of carving by Grinling Gibbons: the wooden altarpiece and the marble font showing Adam and Eve under the Tree of Paradise. The church was severely damaged by enemy action in 1940, and it is interesting to note that when a new spire and weathervane were dropped on to the church by a giant crane in 1968, they were constructed in twentieth-century glass fibre, though the architect and the constructor worked from Wren's original plans for the church.

All the fashionable people wanted to live in the houses which had

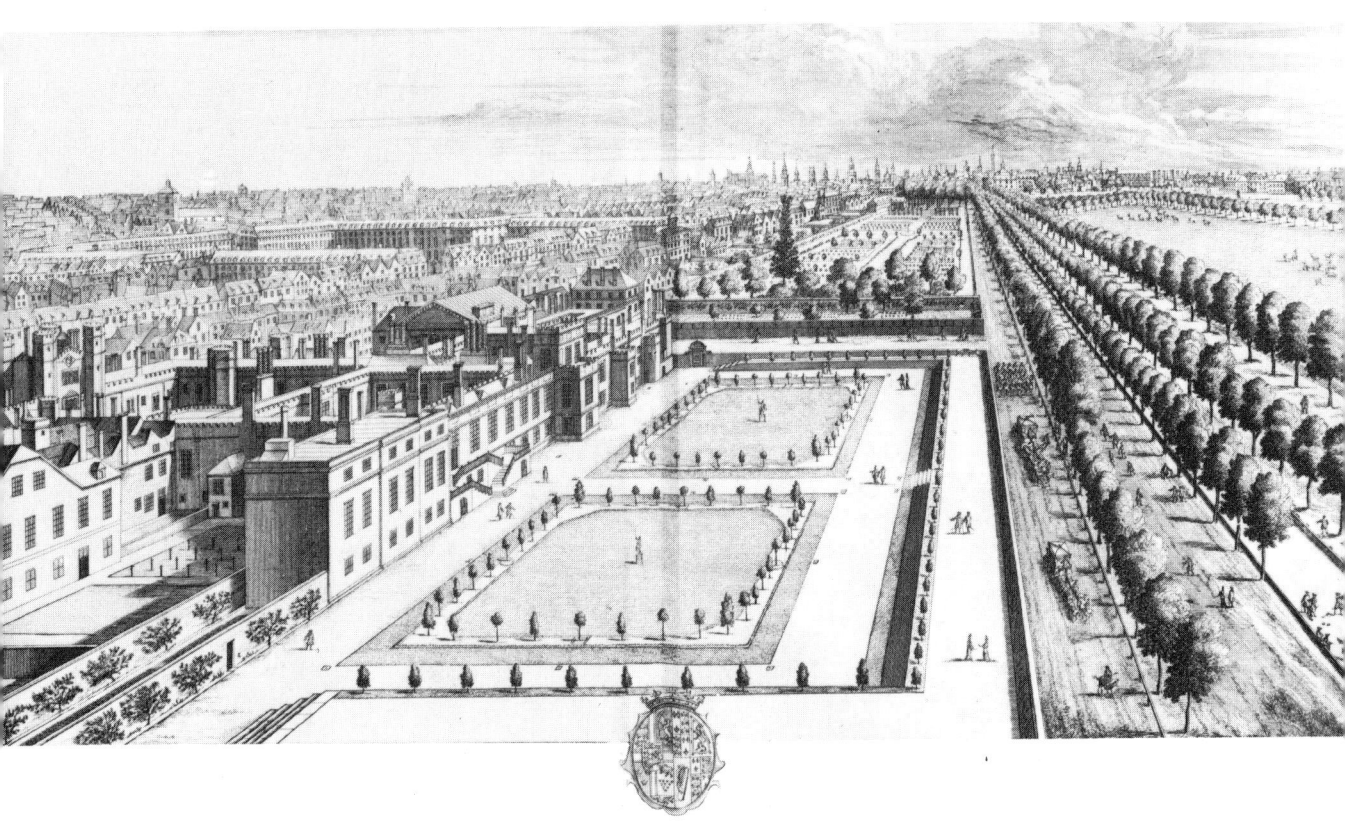

gardens backing on to the Mall, because Charles had his original Pall Mall moved slightly to the south and west, and these houses thus enjoyed an uninterrupted view across the Park of St James. Charles's favourite, Nell Gwynn, had a house there, and would talk to the King over the garden wall as he passed by on his walk, according to John Evelyn who happened to be with the King on one such occasion.

PICCADILLY

The name Piccadilly was applied first to a large house built at the end of the sixteenth century near the windmill (Windmill Street exists today) in the area of what we know as Piccadilly Circus. It was built for a local tailor and collar-maker called Baker and, because it is sometimes said that he made a certain kind of ruff known as a 'Pickadill', the house was called Pickadill House which soon gave its name to the whole area.

Other noblemen began building themselves mansions along the north side of Piccadilly; the Earl of Clarendon built Clarendon House

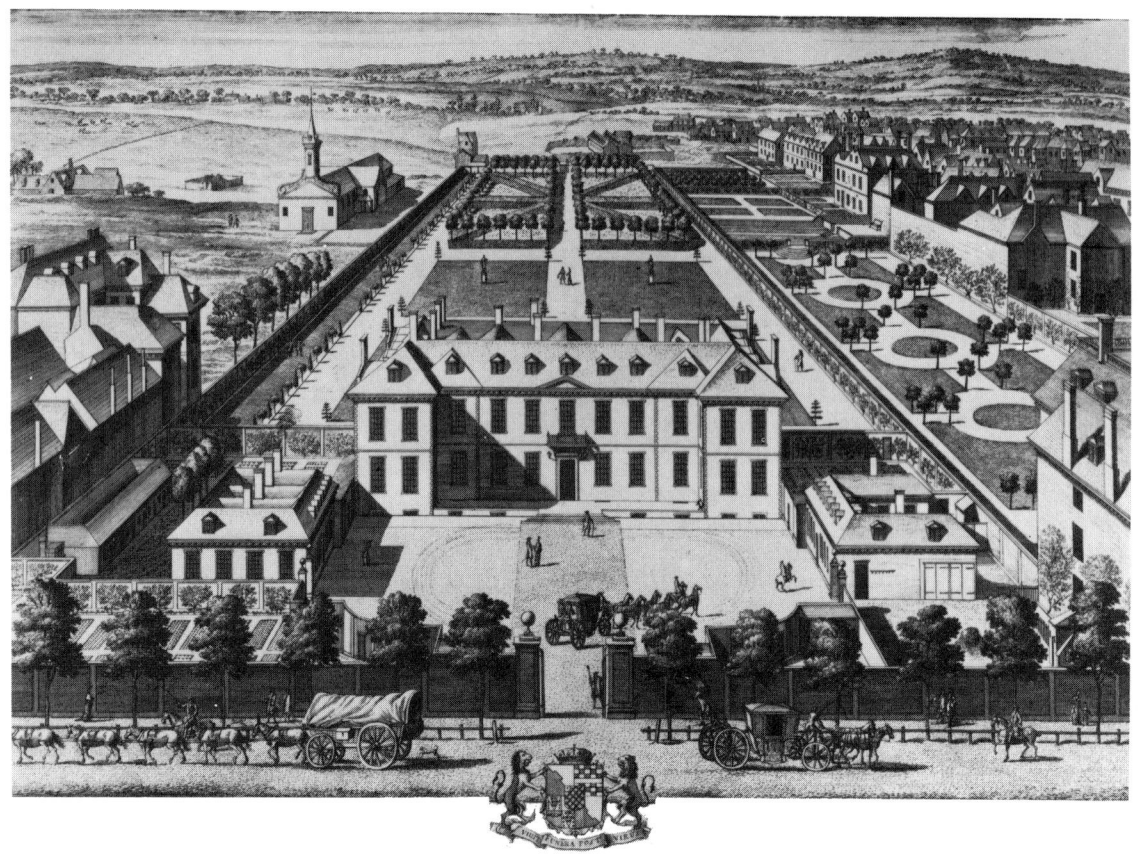

on land he was given by the King. Some of the more cynical Londoners called it Dunkirk House because they said he got it for arranging the sale of Dunkirk back to the French in a secret negotiation made by Charles with Louis XIV. He sold some of his land to Lord Berkeley, Earl of Stratton, and Lord Burlington who built Berkeley House and Burlington House.

Burlington House, Piccadilly, built in 1663–1668, engraving by J. Kip after L. Knyff.

BLOOMSBURY

In the north, Bloomsbury, built around Bloomsbury Square, was developed by the Earl of Southampton, the son of the Earl who had been the patron of Shakespeare in the previous century. He built houses, shops and a market, and, as the air was considered to be very healthy, he had no trouble in letting his property. He died without sons, and his land and wealth passed to his daughter who had married the son of the 4th Earl of Bedford who had built Covent Garden. She and her husband decided to move to Bloomsbury on the death of her father, so they left their house in the Strand and took up residence in Southampton House in Bloomsbury, altering its name to Bedford House. And that is the reason why there are some streets bearing names relating to both the Southampton and Bedford families in both places e.g. Russell Street, Southampton Street and Bedford Street in the Strand area and Great Russell Street, Bedford Row and Southampton Row in the Bloomsbury area.

SOHO

The Master of the Royal Mint, Mr Thomas Neale, developed land east of Piccadilly Hall, basing the development on what was then called Monmouth Square after the Duke of Monmouth. Earlier, this had been a place for hunting and the fields round about had resounded to the call of 'So Hoe!' Later, after the ill-starred Monmouth Rebellion and the consequent execution of the Duke, it was known as King Square, and we know it today as Soho Square. The Earl of Macclesfield and Sir Francis Compton both bought property in this part of London and both have streets named after them.

NICHOLAS BARBON, SPECULATOR

Thomas Neale was one of the first commoners to involve himself in the development of London, but he was far outmatched by Doctor Nicholas Barbon. Barbon's father had been a leatherseller by trade, but he was also a lay preacher of some renown; his full name was If-Jesus-Christ-Had-Not-Died-For-Thee-Thou-Hadst-Been-Damned Barebone. This was generally abbreviated to 'Damned Barebone' and, since he was a good Parliamentarian, he was elected to Cromwell's parliament which became known as the 'Barebones' Parliament. His son, Nicholas, was born about 1640. He was a good scholar and won a place at Leyden University in Holland where he read medicine and economics. He took a medical degree at Utrecht in 1661 and returned to become an Honorary Fellow of the College of Physicians in 1664.

After the Great Fire, Nicholas Barbon, as he now called himself, came into his own, or perhaps we should say into other people's money. He became the first of the great speculators in London property. He began immediately after the Fire by rebuilding his father's house, which he was legally permitted and encouraged to do, but he managed to build on a larger scale than before. Then he moved his old father out into a rented house in Shoe Lane for £25 a year, and let the family house for a much larger sum.

Immediately after the Fire he began the first fire insurance, the 'Phoenix Life Insurance', which was Barbon's one good idea to withstand the test of time. Timber houses cost twice as much to insure as brick and stone ones.

He was unscrupulous in the way he obtained money to invest in property. He borrowed, built, put the money he got from the sale of his houses back into more building, forgot to pay his creditors and built again. He bought Essex House in the Strand with its gardens facing the river. Charles II himself wished to buy it, but while negotiations were going on Barbon, in true speculator's style, demolished the house and began to build. He put up a street of cheaply-made, standardized brick houses there, with a row of warehouses along the riverfront. These were screened from the houses by a brick archway. The street is there today, but nothing remains of Barbon's houses, except the arch which has been restored but still looks more or less as it originally was.

Barbon built over five acres in Spitalfield in the east of London in the same year in which he finally obtained, through careful scheming, a forty-six-year lease on a large part of Soho Fields. Everybody seemed to go down before Barbon like ninepins. When his swift talking and impressive appearance failed, he won through by sheer cheek and daring. But he met an organized resistance from the legal gentlemen of Gray's Inn when he set out to build on Red Lion Fields which were next door to them. They were determined that Barbon's closely packed,

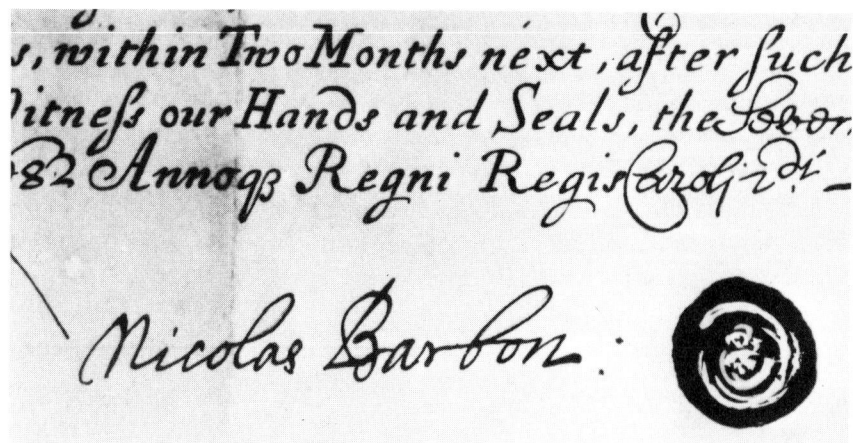

Nicholas Barbon's signature on a Fire Insurance Certificate for the year 1682.

narrow-fronted houses, which quickly deteriorated into slum dwellings, sometimes with a family of more than six to a room, should not spoil their neighbourhood.

The lawyers marched in protest to the fields where they were assailed by furious builder's men. At night they organized commando parties to steal out and knock down as much as possible of what the builders had put up the day before. There were pitched battles and, during one of these, the lawyers took hostages back to Gray's Inn and Barbon was forced to parley. He marched round the square, followed by a number of his workmen chanting slogans, and threatened to bring out a thousand more against the lawyers. But, in the end, he was forced to leave an open space in the middle of his property owing to the lawyer's superior knowledge of the rights of the case. There have been many unscrupulous speculators in London since, unfortunately, but Dr Nicholas Barbon was the pioneer. In his will, game to the last, he left a proviso that none of his debts should be paid.

SHOPS AND MARKETS

The fashionable shops had moved from Cheapside to the Strand, particularly to the New Exchange, where bookshops were now also to be found, as well as around the expensive area of Covent Garden. Also in this quarter were the first coffee-houses which were rapidly taking the place of the Elizabethan taverns for the meeting-place of wits and intelligent men, and those who came to gawp at them.

The old craft quarters were disappearing, but certain goods were still to be found in certain places, such as linen-drapers' wares and jewellery which were to be found in Fleet Street. It was a wealthy jeweller of Fleet Street, Sir Francis Child, who introduced banking to London just after the beginning of the reign of William and Mary, in 1690. He had begun as a jeweller's apprentice and later married the heiress to a firm of rich goldsmiths. Then, in true Dick Whittington style, he became Lord Mayor. While he had been a goldsmith, jeweller and pawnbroker, he had looked after other people's money for them in his house in Fleet Street, and among his customers were people such as Prince Rupert of the Rhine and Nell Gwynne. After 1690 his business was known as Child's Bank, and it exists as a private banking firm today. This was an important new aspect of commerce in London, and one which was to bring in an enormous amount of trade. Until then, the Italians in Lombardy had been the leaders in this world, but London was soon to

overtake them as other banks were set up and patronised by foreign
visitors as well as by royalty and wealthy nobles and citizens.

If the fashionable bookshops were to be found in the New Exchange,
second-hand bookshops were all together in Monmouth Street,
together with the second-hand clothes shops. Mercers' shops were still
in Cheapside and milliners' shops were in both the old Royal and the
New Exchanges. The merchants met on the Royal Exchange, or 'on
'Change' as they called it, as they had done since Elizabeth's time. The
lawyers still studied and practised in the Inns of Courts and, although
the coffee-houses were fashionable meeting-places for the growing
middle class, the taverns were still used for social and convivial
purposes by the working men.

Covent Garden was the main market for fruit and vegetables, the
Leaden Hall was the chief market for beef, mutton was to be bought in
Newgate and veal in St James's market, while cheese was to be found in
the shops in Thames Street.

*A London Coffee-house from
a Broadside of 1674. The coffee
is drunk from bowls, not cups.
Note the bunch of ribbons on
the shoulder of the figure
sitting at the end of the table
on the left: it was a
fashionable fad of the time.*

THE GOVERNMENT OF LONDON

Although trade varied with the ups and downs of the French and Dutch
wars, it was basically sound and, as the nobility left the City, so it
became more and more the merchants' own private kingdom. Yet
Charles II treated the City in as contemptuous a fashion as his father had
done; he went further – he withdrew its Charter of rights and privileges
when he could not get his own way in 1682. He later offered to return it,
provided he had his say in the election of the Lord Mayor and
Aldermen. The Common Council of London refused, and so the City's

government passed into the hands of officers nominated by the King.

After Charles's death, his brother, James II, realized that he needed the support of the City and he returned its Charter. But it was too late; the City might have forgiven, but it did not forget the abuse. When James gave preferment to Catholic officials in the Government and universities, it decided that the time had arrived for James to go. The Catholic religion, with its echo of Spanish conquest, had always been a source of fear for the Londoner, and nothing was easier than to stir up the London apprentices by raising the cry of 'No Popery!' So, in 1688, London welcomed William, Prince of Orange, who was to share the throne with his wife, James's daughter, Mary.

William and Mary did little to alter the face of London which was still being rebuilt; they were more concerned with their two palaces of Hampton Court and Kensington and, to a slightly lesser degree, the palace at Greenwich. William preferred to live out of the capital because, it is thought, he was subject to asthma and needed the cleaner air to be found outside London. Sir Christopher Wren added a new east front in the Renaissance style to Hampton Court, two large wings to the complex he had already begun at Greenwich, and enlarged Kensington House, which William had bought from the Earl of Nottingham in 1689, in a style which is slightly reminiscent of the Dutch atmosphere to which the King had been accustomed.

Kensington House or Kensington Palace as it was henceforth known, was also a favourite residence of Queen Anne (1702–1714), who, now that White Hall Palace had been burned down in the previous reign of William and her sister Mary, did not reside in the capital at all. She was a devout supporter of the Anglican High Church and was convinced that a growing population needed more churches. So in 1711, Parliament approved the plan for the building of fifty-one new churches, although only a handful of these were actually built. Wren's brilliant assistant and pupil, Nicholas Hawksmoor, designed six of them: in the east, St Anne's, Limehouse, Christchurch in Spitalfield and St George in the East; in the expanding suburbs: St Alphege's in Greenwich and St George's in Bloomsbury; in the City itself, St Mary Woolnoth. Today, restored but still beautiful, they remain.

A Coffee-plant and a Vine.

5
London's 'new look'

QUITE literally, a great wind of change blew through London at the beginning of Queen Anne's reign, for the morning of 26 November 1703 was the morning of the hurricane known as the Great Storm. The wind blew hard all day and increased at night; the mercury sank in the barometers lower than had ever been seen before. An eye-witness wrote: 'It did not blow so hard, till twelve o'clock at night, but that most families went to bed, though many of them with some concern at the terrible wind; but about one, or at least by two, few people that were capable of any sense of danger, were so hardy as to lie in bed; the fury of the tempest increased to such a degree, that most people expected the fall of their houses.

'And yet, in this general apprehension, nobody durst quit their tottering habitations; for whatever the danger was within doors, it was worse without; the bricks, tiles, and stones, from the tops of the houses, flew with such force, and so thick in the streets, that no one thought fit to venture out, though their houses were nearly demolished.

'Such a shock was given to a well-built brick house in the skirts of the city, by a stack of chimnies falling on the next houses, that the inhabitants imagined it was coming down on their heads. . . .'

The storm increased in fury and blew to its highest pitch at six

Queen Anne (1702–1714), the last of the reigning Stuarts. Detail from a painting attributed to Michael Dahl.

o'clock the following morning. Ships on the Thames were blown from their moorings and crashed into each other; between Shadwell and Limehouse 700 ships lay piled into heaps, their hulls stove in and their masts and spars like so much tinder. It was estimated that 2000 chimney stacks were blown down; the streets were covered with slates and tiles and, it was said, twenty houses were blown down completely. The eye-witness's reference to a 'well-built brick house' indicates that there were some which were not well-built, and there must have been some old lathe and plaster houses which disappeared in the hurricane. Westminster Abbey lost the lead off its roof, as did a number of other churches. Two hundred people were estimated to have been injured and some thirty or forty killed. The devastation was immense.

In 1688, there had been an upset in the affairs of the country of an equal magnitude: the 'Glorious Revolution' – glorious because it spilt no blood – replaced the Catholic James II with his Protestant daughter, Mary, and her Dutch Protestant husband, William of Orange, jointly on the throne of England. The Londoners supported the new monarchs as they did James's second daughter, Anne, who succeeded in 1702 and the first of the Georges who came over from Hanover to take the throne in 1714, because they did not want the Catholic Stuarts. Trade and industry in London were better than ever, and the practical citizens saw no reason to upset this happy state of affairs: they preferred settled order. Although England was at war during a large part of the eighteenth century, these battles in France, Spain, the German states and the Lowlands were a long way away, and did little to disturb the even character of life at home, apart from making demands on its pocket.

BANK OF ENGLAND

Such demands in William's reign led to the National Debt which, incidentally, has never been repaid, and to the establishment of the Bank of England. A syndicate of wealthy merchants including, of course, some goldsmiths, was formed to raise and lend the sum of £1 200 000. The syndicate was led by a Scotsman, William Paterson, and it was given a royal charter and title of the Bank of England. From 1695 to 1734, when it moved to a new building in the same street, the Bank occupied the Grocer's Hall in Threadneedle Street. Later, other banks received charters, but the Bank of England had the monopoly of lending only to the nation, and not to the general public.

63

It is difficult for us today to imagine how London must have looked to the Londoners after the Fire. Everything would have been new – the Wren churches and St Paul's in the process of being built – the Cathedral in gleaming white stone, the Monument in white marble crowned with gold flames, the rebuilt Guildhall and the new, flat-fronted, sash-windowed houses.

A bracket clock, engraved with silver, made in London by Donald Bouquet.

A gradual change, which had begun in Charles II's reign and reached its height in that of Queen Anne, was also bringing a new look to the appearance of society. The nobility still remained and, although they kept more or less to the fashionable quarters of St James, Knightsbridge and Bloomsbury, they were at least visible. In Elizabeth's time, they had kept themselves to their large mansions on the London river which they entered from their barges, and to the royal palaces; they were rarely to be seen on foot in the capital. Charles II had made a habit of walking with his courtiers in Pall Mall, and of feeding the ducks in St James's Park; during the Great Fire he walked among his people, encouraging them. He had had 'the common touch' which his brother, James II, William and Mary and Anne lacked. Nevertheless, although the nobility was to be seen going about the town, it did not mix socially with anyone outside its own society.

The new middle class developed, as it were, at both ends. The top layer consisted of the new professional people, headed by the architects who had come into prominence during the rebuilding of London: men such as Sir Christopher Wren, Nicholas Hawksmoor and Sir John Vanburgh who was also a well-known dramatist. These were the friends of royalty and nobility. Doctors of medicine or science and of letters were treated with respect, as were lawyers, the higher military ranks and the richer type of clergymen and the leading merchants. All these, and others, formed the new upper middle class.

At the other end of this section were the poor clergy, shopkeepers and people such as druggists, or chemists as we should call them now, and scriveners who wrote letters for people – and there were thousands of them – who could not write themselves. This was the lower middle class, and between the upper and the lower, there was as great a distinction as there was between the aristocracy and the upper middle bracket.

This difference in status was symbolized by the areas of London in which they lived. The well-born and the very rich lived in the west and Bloomsbury, the very poor lived in the east, in Spitalfields,

Whitechapel and Limehouse, and the two classes were separated by the Inns of Court and dwellings of the legal profession, stretching up from the river at the Temple, through Lincoln and Gray's Inns to Red Lion Square, and by the well-to-do, fashionable middle-class area of Covent Garden. For ever afterwards, the class structure of London was fixed.

Apart from the difference in their income and the area in which they lived, the other visible mark of distinction between one Londoner and another was dress. The upper and middle class throughout the eighteenth century wore more or less the same kind of dress, but the difference lay in the richness of the materials and the extravagances of the decoration. England had been famed since medieval times for the quality of her woollen manufacture and other cloths, and this was still one of London's greatest exports. Much silk had been imported from France and Italy but, gradually, as the Spitalfields weaving trade increased so the fashionable ladies and gentlemen took to wearing English silk.

WIGS FOR MEN

The greatest innovation in fashion which was common to all classes and lasted through most of the eighteenth century was that of the wig. Its use began around the beginning of the reign of Charles II. Charles himself had very luxuriant dark hair, and neither he nor his brother adopted the wig when it first came in. But on 2 November 1663, Pepys overheard the Duke of York say that he was going to wear a periwig, and said that there was a rumour that the King would do so as well. He added: 'I have never till this day observed that the King is mighty grey'. The next day he had the wig-maker, one Chapman, come to see him and, not without misgiving, had his own hair cut off and bought a periwig which cost him £3, worth a great deal more in those days. He also had his own hair made up into another wig. When he put the wig on, his maids thought it became him, so he went out to a coffee-house and met his friend, Sir William Penn, the Quaker leader who was to found the American state of Pennsylvania. Sir William was very interested and talked much about the step Pepys had taken, 'as he do of every thing that concerns me, but it is over, and so I perceive after a day or two it will be no great matter.' But he was still secretly worried about his wig for, on Sunday, 8 November, he wore it to church, 'and there I found that my coming in a periwig did not prove so strange to the world as I was afeard it would, for I thought that all the church would

A fine example of a full-bottomed wig worn by Anthony Ashley, second Earl of Shaftesbury. Miniature by Samuel Cooper.

presently have cast their eyes all upon me, but I found no such thing.'

The long, curling, luxuriant periwigs had been the fashion in France for some little time, but in England they may have been adopted both as a reaction against the close crops of the Roundheads as well as a measure of cleanliness. False hairpieces may have been added to sparse locks at the time of the Restoration in case anyone thought that a man with a little hair might be a Roundhead. It was a short step from false hairpieces to full periwigs. We have remarked before on the dirtiness of London at this time and on the lack of facilities for both private and public hygiene which we nowadays take for granted. So it was a very common thing for people to find lice in their long hair and the parasites were easily transferred from one person to another. The head could therefore be kept clean by the regular shaving which was necessary if a wig was to be worn in comfort. Some men kept their hair fairly short under the wig, and wore it without a wig when at home. A man with a shaved head would normally wear a soft cap of silk or velvet, if he could afford it, though only in his own surroundings.

The colours of the wigs varied from blond through light brown and chestnut to black. Few grey wigs were seen among the fashionable men and, for a bald-headed man, the wig was a godsend. Thus it was also possible to disguise age to some degree. During the early years of the Restoration, the wig was long and full on the shoulders and flat on top. Soon after 1670 or so, it began to rise on top until it was almost triangular in shape. By the turn of the century it was usually parted in the middle and twisted into two horns on either side. Such wigs were heavy and cumbersome and had to be pulled off in a hurry if any strenuous activity, such as a duel, occurred. Shorter, full-bottomed wigs arrived and both these as well as the longer periwigs were worn all through Queen Anne's reign. The bob wig was worn by all kinds of people for informal wear from about the turn of the century, and this

The periwig, circa 1700.

reached either to just below the ears or to just above the shoulders. About the same time, the bag wig was fashionable for informal wear, especially for young men, and this meant drawing the hair back and confining it in a black silken bag drawn in by a bow. There was also the campaign wig, favoured for military matters or for travelling; for this the hair was divided into three parts, one on each side and one at the back, and the ends were turned up and tied with a small bow or knot to keep them out of the way.

'Spring', from 'The Seasons', etched by Wenceslas Hollar about 1641. The dress is typical of that worn by a well-to-do young girl of the period.

WOMEN'S CLOTHES

Women's clothes kept roughly the shape that they had had in Elizabeth's time, with the great exception of the wide, stiffened skirt which the court ladies wore – the farthingale. Skirts fell more naturally, without stiffening, from the waist, and the bodice, although still close-fitting, was not quite so tightly laced. Nor, except for the ladies of the Court, was the low-cut gown much to be seen in London, and certainly not among the wives of the merchants and traders. The basic pattern of dress for women during the whole of the Stuart period which ended with Anne's death, was for a close-fitting bodice with sleeves of varying widths to the elbow, where they were usually edged with lace, and a wide skirt which often opened down the middle over an under-petticoat either embroidered or of a different colour.

Women's hair was dressed flat on top and very frizzed out at the sides during the Jacobean period, with ringlets at the sides during the reign of Charles I, and with slightly longer curls falling on to their shoulders in that of Charles II. After about 1690, they began to wear high structures of wired lace and ribbon on their heads, and this fashion lasted for at least a decade. Then they wore their hair much more piled up on the top of the head, with a curl or two falling on to the shoulders.

Ruffs became smaller during James's reign and turned firstly into the wide lace collar of the Cavalier, or the plain white starched Puritan collar, and then into the lace cravat or the plain white linen cravat of the Restoration period. Ladies of the Court, or of wealthy means, wore a filmy kerchief to cover their bare shoulders, while the neckline of their dresses might also have a lace edging. The middle-class woman would wear her dress close to the throat with, perhaps, a lace collar, or at least a fine linen one. Her head would be covered with a hood when she went out, and both men and women covered themselves against the winter cold with voluminous cloaks.

During the reign of the first Stuart king clothes had developed from the Tudor doublet, breeches and hose into a longer doublet, often with a kind of skirt formed of loops of the material or of ribbon, longer and puffier breeches and stockings which terminated in flat-heeled shoes decorated with rosettes or pompoms of silk or lace.

French court-dress usually set the fashion for that of London, at least until the Restoration. In the centre of this engraving after Le Blond, is King Louis XIII (1610–1643) with his queen, Anne of Austria.

68

*A Cavalier's dress, circa
1640.*

The fashionable Londoner's hat had changed from the conical felt worn at the beginning of the seventeenth century, such as those we see in drawings of the Guy Fawkes' conspirators to the wide-brimmed, flatter-crowned model in vogue after the Restoration. During Charles I's reign, the tendency was for men's jackets to become slightly longer, with less puffy breeches fastening at the knee, worn with rich lace collars, while the jacket began to get a less fussy look. More depended on material and style than upon the peacock-coloured, brilliantly decorated clothes of the Tudor man. On 13 October 1666, Charles II altered the style of men's clothes forever afterwards. He declared officially that he was going to wear a long 'vest' or waistcoat, in the Persian style, and, said Pepys, 'he will be in it for good and all on Monday next and the whole Court: it is a fashion, the King says, he will never change.' And, sure enough on the following Monday, 15 October, the King put on his new waistcoat and a number of courtiers and members of Parliament as well: 'being a long cassock close to the body, of black cloth, and pinked with white silk under it, and a coat over it, and the legs ruffled with black riband like a pigeon's leg: and upon the whole I wish the King may keep it, for it is a very fine and handsome garment,' decided Pepys. Thus clad, with a wide-brimmed, luxuriantly feathered hat, and on fairly high heels, with perhaps a staff to help him in his progress, the fashionable London gentleman would venture forth to take the air. All this made for dignity: a velvet or heavy silk coat and breeches, a heavy wig and large hat with feathers made a man move ponderously and carefully.

*This engraving of the
conspirators in the Gunpowder
Plot, 1605, shows clearly how
men dressed in the early years
of the reign of James I.*

Dignity, too, belonged to the average City merchant who rebuilt his house after the Great Fire in solid brick and stone, and went on living solidly in the City in the way his father had done before him. He lived and carried on his business in the same house, soberly dressed in a long jacket which reached to his knees. This covered a white cambric shirt and breeches held in by a band below his knees above dark-coloured shoes and stockings. The shoes would probably have silver buckles. At the time of the Restoration men wore far less jewellery, even among the nobility, than they had during the reigns of Elizabeth and James I. Round the London merchant's neck would be a white linen stock and, during this period, white linen began to be a mark of distinction and became the outward sign of a gentleman. He would also wear a broad-brimmed hat, but with dark feathers, if any. He did not go in for ostentatious display, but neither did he abjure all ornament as the Puritans had done, so it was likely that his waistcoat might be discreetly laced with silver, or embroidered in coloured threads. The skirts of his womenfolk would be as full as those of the ladies of the Court, but their shoulders would be more discreetly covered, and their hair not quite so elaborately curled as the coiffures to be seen in Pall Mall.

Gradually, during Anne's reign, the long overcoat worn by men gave way to the full-skirted shorter coat, with wide cuffs, in silk or velvet and heavily embroidered down the fronts of the coat, worn with knee breeches. The wide brim of the hat was turned up, at first on one, and then on all three sides and developed into the tricorne which remained the gentleman's headgear for the rest of the eighteenth century. Swords were worn during Anne's reign, with special 'dress' swords for wear on important social occasions, and a walking stick was also frequently carried. Add to this a snuffbox, and you can see that the fashionable 'beau' or fop of Queen Anne's time literally had his hands full if he wanted to cut a fashionable figure.

A silver snuff-box with a design of a London street-scene.

THE POOR

What of the poor of London? As usual with poor in all ages and in all countries, fashion meant nothing to them: they needed clothes as a protection against the elements and when they could not buy them new, they either bought them secondhand or relied on charity. During the eighteenth century, the secondhand clothes market was in Monmouth Street, a street still to be found in the area we know now as Cambridge Circus. A wig was handed down from the gentleman to his valet, then

70

down through the footmen until it was finally sold in Monmouth Street to grace the head of some poor man who could not afford better. The last stage for a wig was to be used as a polisher for shining shoes by the shoe-blacks who were very necessary in a city as dirty and muddy as London.

APPRENTICES

Another poor citizen of London was the apprentice. His appearance was roughly the same as his master with regard to the style of his clothes – the short doublet, longer breeches developing into the longer jacket and knee-breeches as the century wore on, but the materials of which his clothes were made were rough and shoddy, unless he was fortunate enough to have a kind mercer for a master who might be inclined to spare him a little of his less expensive cloth at cost price! His round, flat woollen cap had disappeared and a low-crowned, fairly wide-brimmed and completely unadorned felt seemed to take its place. The laws governing the dress and behaviour of the apprentices were upheld by the various guilds as firmly as they had been in the time of Elizabeth, even though the power of the guilds themselves was beginning to diminish in the reign of Anne.

A chimney-sweep and his apprentice in the second half of the seventeenth century.

6
Domestic life and leisure

THE new flat-fronted, sash-windowed houses built on two, three or occasionally four floors were practical places to live in. On the ground floor there would probably be the hall, dining-room and kitchen and perhaps a sitting-room. On the first floor a man such as Pepys would have his study, and his wife her boudoir or 'closet'; on the floor above in a three-storeyed house, there would be one or two bedrooms and a dressing-room, with servants' quarters in the attic rooms in the roof. In the wealthier, larger houses, the sitting-room, or 'withdrawing-room' would be situated on the first floor, with a wide staircase leading up to that floor from the hall.

FURNITURE

There was more furniture in the rooms than there had been in the Tudor and Jacobean periods. The main bedroom would have a wooden bedstead, quite often richly carved, with a canopy and curtains and a valance round the bottom of the bed, all in some rich, thick material, such as velvet or damask. There would be a chest to store linen and a good supply of blankets, a looking-glass and three or four heavily-

A flat-fronted London House, circa 1700.

A Queen Anne settee and chair in walnut, upholstered in tapestry, circa 1690.

carved chairs. In September 1668 Pepys and his wife decided to refurnish their living quarters in the Navy Office Building in Seething Lane near the Tower, so he took her and her maid, Deb, by coach to St James to see Christopher Wren's bed and hangings, and then to Sir William Coventry's house in Pall Mall for the same reason, to help them make up their minds about the kind of tapestry hangings they should have on their bedroom walls. They decided on a set depicting the Apostles: 'and so by Mr Crow's home, about his hangings, and do pitch upon buying his second suit of Apostles, the whole suit, which comes to £83; and this we think the best for us, having now the whole suit to answer any other rooms or service.'

There would be hangings of leather, probably gilded or embossed, or of velvet in the drawing-room, which helped to keep the bare walls warm, as well as tapestries. Most rooms boasted a set of six chairs upholstered in cloth, a leather-covered chair and a plush armchair, a table and a clock, and one or two footstools. Matting or rushes were to be found on the floor, while wealthier households would proudly display a Turkey carpet as a table covering. Cupboards were beginning to be used instead of chests for storing clothes and other goods, and there was frequently a corner cupboard in the dining-room to hold the wooden platters, pewter tankards and bowls and, in the richer households, the crystal goblets. There were knives of steel with horn handles, but forks were still rather rare.

In most houses breakfast was served around 8 a.m., and usually consisted of cold meat and bread or oat-cake with small beer – the national beverage, and drunk even by children – to accompany it. Tea was a fashionable luxury, and on 28 September 1660 Samuel Pepys noted in his diary: 'I did send for a cup of tee (a China drink) of which I never had drunk before'. Strong beer and various kinds of ale were consumed, and it was not unusual for a man to drink three quarts of beer a day. Wine imported from the Continent was popular among the better-off, and other drinks were coffee, although this was drunk more outside the home than in, cider, mead and brandy.

A Queen Anne silver teapot with warmer.

The Londoner took dinner, his main meal of the day, at any time between one and five o'clock. Although the innumerable courses of the Tudor age had disappeared, people still ate far more than we do now. There was another departure from Tudor custom in that all the courses were no longer placed on the table at once, but one at a time. Again, Pepys – so often the authority for the details of life in Restoration London – records what he had for dinner on 26 January 1661: 'my wife had got ready a very fine dinner – viz. a dish of marrow bones; a leg of mutton; a loin of veal; a dish of fowl, three pullets, and two dozen of larks all in a dish; a great tart, a neat's* tongue, a dish of anchovies; a dish of prawns and cheese. My company was my father, my uncle Fenner, his two sons, Mr Pierce, and all their wives, and my brother Tom.' Much of the meat had to be salted and laid down for use in the winter months, and this also applied to some fish. We know from Pepys's account that he was fond of oysters in season, and of lobster, as well as sturgeon, lampreys (sometimes eaten in a pie), eels and tench.

COMMUNICATIONS

This was a period when Londoners were perhaps more convivial than they are today: they were always making up parties to go to dinners in one another's houses, or taking boats on the river to go for picnics along the south bank, or forming parties to sing madrigals. They kept in touch with one another by sending notes by hand. Letters, valuables and parcels of all kinds were carried by licenced porters of good character who stood at street corners for hire. An attempt at establishing a penny post was made in 1680 by a merchant called

*A neat is an animal of the ox kind – an ox or bullock, cow or heifer (vi Oxford Shorter Dic.).

William Dockwra, to deliver letters and parcels six or eight times a day in the area of the Royal Exchange, and four times a day in the suburbs. The porters did not like the idea, and it was finally suppressed by the Duke of York who had held the monopoly of the National Posts, which had not been very successful, since 1663.

SHOPS

The fashionable shops, with the exception of those in the galleries of the Royal Exchange, had moved west from Cheapside to the Strand, particularly to the New Exchange where there were also bookshops to be found. It was not considered proper for women to walk in the streets even with their maids except in Cheapside, Ludgate Hill or in either of the Exchanges, these being the places where all the busy shops were to be found. Pepys was quite happy to drop his wife off from their coach at the New Exchange while he went about his morning business. The shops were, for the most part, still open to the street as they had been in earlier times: very few of them boasted glass, and nor did they have doors. The apprentice still stood at the doorway calling out the excellence of his master's wares, and the streets were as noisy as they had ever been.

THE RUNNING OF THE HOUSEHOLD

The position of women and children had changed little from that they had held in the previous century. Children were still dressed in smaller versions of adult clothes, and were still very much in submission to their parents. Boys were taught either privately by a tutor at home, as in the wealthier families, or went to a school attached to a church or a specially endowed school. By the age of nine or ten, they were expected to be able to read the classics with a certain ease, and to speak Latin and/or Greek tolerably well; they also, if they were of an upper middle-class family, learned to speak French and had fencing and dancing lessons. They were able to cope with the rudiments of mathematics and geography and to write a legible hand. When they did not perform their lessons well they were soundly whipped, either by their tutor, their father or their schoolmaster. If you were fortunate enough to be a

prince, such as Henry and Charles, the sons of James I, you would have a 'whipping-boy' who earned a reasonably comfortable life at Court in return for taking all the prince's punishments. Girls, with a few exceptions, still received a very scanty formal education, but were practised in the household arts and those of embroidery and singing.

Women ran their households like a small kingdom. Unless you were very poor, you always had domestic help. People of good positions had a number of servants, for there were always many poor people who needed work for which they would be given shelter, food and a pittance of a wage. An alderman or sheriff would have as many as thirty or forty servants in his house in the City, and Pepys, who maintained a modest household, had a cook, housemaid, general maid of all work and a personal maid for his wife. When a lady walked abroad in the street she would be followed by a footman and accompanied by her maid. The apprentice's work included escorting his mistress about her comings and goings in the City. Some gentleman of rank would have two running footmen preceding his carriage, supposedly to announce his arrival in the next town, who would be dressed in white and carrying a cane with a hollow end which contained an orange or a lemon to refresh them during their running.

The ladies of the house during the middle of the eighteenth century would usually sit at the upper end of the table during family meals and help everyone else before themselves. The good housewife also kept a still-room where she prepared various kinds of wines and cordials as well as remedies against the fever and the plague, mostly made from herbs and plants and from recipes handed down from mother to daughter. All this, together with the day-to-day running of her house and the preparation of three meals a day (for there was supper served at 6 p.m. or thereabouts, consisting of cold meat, 'sallet', or salad as we call it, and a tankard of strong ale) as well as the teaching of her daughters and the carrying out of any social function, made the Stuart housewife a very busy woman.

When there was a large social occasion, it was quite often the custom in those households which could afford it to order the food from a cook's shop, and then a procession of cook's assistants carrying various covered dishes containing such delicacies as goose-pie, turkey stuffed with cloves, beef dressed with vinegar and pepper (the old Tudor custom of dressing beef and mutton with honey had disappeared) dates in broth and grapes boiled in butter would be seen following the chief cook in his white apron and cap, bearing aloft a large dish holding a young roasted peacock.

Prince James Francis Edward Stuart, accompanied by his sister, Princess Louise Marie, painted by Nicolas de Largillière in 1695. Children at this period were dressed exactly like their elders.

A London Coffee-house around 1705. Newspapers are much in evidence.

TAVERNS

It was the custom now for many tradesmen to leave the shop to the care of their apprentices while they went to take their midday meal in a nearby tavern. Unmarried men would take most of their meals in a tavern too, and the best-known one was Lockett's at Charing Cross. The taverns were still used for business, as they always had been, and their numbers increased all the time along the two main roads, one leading over the bridge at Southwark right into the heart of the City at Bishopsgate and the other from the Royal Exchange, Cornhill, to the Strand. Besides Lockett's, the other two best-known taverns were the Rose and the Sun. Tradesmen frequented them during the day, and clubs, societies and trade gatherings at night.

COFFEE HOUSES

The man who sought intellectual entertainment for the price of two pence – the cost of a glass of sweet, black coffee – would visit a coffee-house, where he could sit by the fire at one of the little tables and read a newspaper kept for the customers, but fastened to a cane in the same way they are today in cafés in Vienna or elsewhere in Europe. Drinking your 'Politician's Porridge', as the coffee was called, you always had to be prepared to talk if spoken to, but usually, you went to the coffee-house to listen to the discourses of others more witty, learned, or simply more confident than yourself. Pepys on 11 November 1663 reported that he went 'at noon to the Coffee-house, where with Dr Allen some good discourse about physicks and chymistry. And among other things, I telling him what Dribble the German Doctor do offer of an instrument to sink ships; he tells me that which is more strange that something made of gold, which they call in chymistry *Aurum Fulminans*, a grain, I think he said, of it put into a silver spoon and fired, will give a blow like a musquett, and strike a hole through the silver spoon downwards, without the least force upward; and this he can make a cheaper experiment of, he says, with iron prepared.'

The first coffee-house was opened by a Greek in 1652 on Cornhill, and the fashion caught on. There were said to be five hundred of them in London in Queen Anne's time, and eight thousand by the end of the century. It rapidly became a habit for men to visit the coffee-house once, twice or even thrice daily and, as the period after dinner in the afternoon was often the recreational period for busy men, who went back to their offices, as Pepys was wont to do, for an hour or two's work in the early evening, there was usually a large clientele in the late afternoons. The object was not only to drink coffee but also to exchange conversation and points of view. While the newspaper industry was still in its infancy, the coffee-house acted as a kind of clearing centre for news and business. The Stock Exchange grew out of coffee-house origins, from two houses, in fact, called Jonathan's and Garraway's, both of which were situated in 'Change Alley, by the Royal Exchange'. Men with shipping and trading interests visited Lloyd's Coffee-house which was one of the oldest of them all, as it was opened in Tower Street in 1688. Its owner, Edward Lloyd, used to paste shipping news on the walls of his premises because this was not given in the newspapers. Later, he brought out *Lloyd's News* for that purpose, and replaced that with *Lloyd's List* in 1734 which has remained the authoritative bulletin on shipping ever since. More important still, Lloyd's has remained as the greatest marine insurance agency in the world.

Will's Coffee-house, in the fashionable Covent Garden area, was the meeting-place of famous literary men, such as Dryden, Addison, Steele and later, Swift. Pepys was thrilled to have been there as he recorded on 3 February 1664: 'In Covent Garden tonight, going to fetch my wife, I stopped at the great Coffee-house there, where I never was before: where Dryden the poet (I knew at Cambridge) and all the wits of the town and Harris the player, and Mr Hoole of our College. And had I

A detail from G. Kneller's portrait of Sir Richard Steel (1672–1729), essayist and dramatist. He was editor of 'The Tatler' 1709 and co-editor with Joseph Addison of 'The Spectator' in 1711.

79

had time then, or could at other times, it will be good coming thither, for there I perceive, is very witty and pleasant discourse. But I could not tarry, and as it was late, they were all ready to go away.'

Later in Anne's reign, Will's still retained its literary atmosphere, while booksellers gathered at the Chapter, as did their authors. The two political parties which were gathering power during her reign were the Tories, who were inclined to the old established order and the Church of England and who contained some Jacobites or followers of the exiled son of James II, and the Whigs, who were the more progressive of the two, being composed of the new landed gentry and the rich merchants. The Tories, and particularly the Jacobites, favoured the Cocoa Tree, while the Whigs went to the St James's. Lawyers and scholars met at Nando's in Inner Temple Lane, and the brightest of the wits went to Will's, Button's or the Smyrna. Frenchmen visiting London went to the St Giles to meet other Frenchmen, and Scots went to the British Coffee-house. Every type of man had his own coffee-house. Great men, such as John Dryden, sat enthroned in their particular corner, and held forth to an admiring circle and woe betide any ignorant newcomer who interrupted the flow of such a great man's talk!

The great popularity of the coffee-house made it a place of tremendous influence in times of political agitation and, because of this, the King tried to get them suppressed in 1675, but with no success. Some coffee-houses were less serious and offered songs and music as their main attraction.

CHOCOLATE HOUSES

Chocolate-houses seemed to have a less serious clientele – or perhaps the same clientele as the coffee-houses, but in a less serious mood. They were pretty places, beautifully painted with lots of gilding and looking-glasses and delicate chairs and tables. People were less inclined to smoke here than they were in the coffee-houses where the glass of coffee was nearly always accompanied by a long pipe of tobacco.

CLUBS

Out of the coffee-houses grew the clubs. In fact, they grew out of the same circles within the coffee-house itself, but they were more exclusive. No one could attend a meeting of a club without being invited. In the coffee-house or chocolate-house, only coffee or chocolate were served, but in the club a man could get through as many bottles of wine or glasses of punch as he fancied. Some clubs were more convivial than others, and existed mainly for eating or drinking, like the Beefsteak Club; others were simply for discussing the arts or politics. Many clubs existed solely on and for gambling, such as White's, which was originally a chocolate-house founded in 1693, and which was favoured by fashionable Tories. A Mr Almack, who owned the Thatched House Tavern in St James's Street, founded Almack's Club which he later sold to a Mr Brooke, and there, and in Boodle's Club, also in St James's Street, were to be found exclusive nightly gatherings of the nobility and the very rich. Thousands of pounds were gambled away nightly.

THE KIT KAT CLUB

The Kit Kat Club, founded in 1700, and which may or may not have been called after a certain kind of mutton pie sold there, was frequented by Whigs. The original founders were thirty-nine noblemen and gentlemen, and their portraits, painted to hang on the Club walls, may be seen today in the National Portrait Gallery. After Queen Anne's death, the Whigs supported the Hanoverian claimant to the throne, Prince George. Among the Whigs of the Kit Kat were Sir Robert Walpole, who was to become our first 'Prime' Minister, the dramatist Vanburgh (who was also the architect of the splendid palace at Blenheim), the essayist Joseph Addison, and many other men of letters and learning.

NEWSPAPERS

A London Gazette seller, circa 1650.

Men went to their favourite coffee-house or club to exchange views and the news of the day, but the first news-sheet to bear a resemblance to a newspaper as we know it today was *The Weekly News from Italy, Germany, etc.* which appeared in May 1622. The editors were Nicholas Bourne and Thomas Archer. Soon afterwards Nathaniel Butter brought out *News from Most Parts of Christendom*, and eventually the two papers were fused into a joint production entitled *News of the Present Week*. It was not published every week, however, but it was the first news-sheet to come out in a more or less continuous form. Also in 1622, the *London Weekly Courant* appeared. In 1638 Charles I gave Nathaniel Butter permission to publish foreign news on payment of £10 a year which was to go towards the repair of St Paul's Cathedral; this was another of the ingenious schemes to which Charles turned for raising money, although this time it was in a worthy cause. In 1663 *Kingdom's Intelligence* was published, and it was incorporated with the *London Gazette* in 1665.

Some of the most famous newspapers were Daniel Defoe's *The Review* which came out three times a week between 1704 and 1713, *The Tatler* edited by Richard Steele in 1709, and *The Spectator* brought out by Steele and Joseph Addison in 1711. The chief Tory paper was *The Examiner*, and Swift wrote its leading articles. The numbers of the papers increased and, by 1711, one official source claimed that there were 44000 copies printed weekly. Even allowing for some exaggeration, there certainly seems to have been a great number, and the Government began to realize the power of the press; it began to subsidize newspapers to carry its points of view, and people began to pay for advertisements to be placed in them. A new London industry had been born.

7

'The Spirit
of the Age'

F R O M what we read of the weather of seventeenth- and eighteenth-
century London, it was much more intense – summers were a great
deal warmer and winters much fiercer. The Thames was frozen over on
a number of occasions and, when this happened in 1608, five years after
the accession of James 1, a magnificent Frost Fair was staged on the ice.
James was staying at his palace at Greenwich when the river began to
freeze, and he thought that it would make a great diversion for both the
Court and the people if he transferred his majesty to the ice. So tents and
marquees, lined and carpeted with furs, were set up for the Court.
James reigned in state from a special throne, and a silken cord was
strung around a large area of the ice to mark off the private territory
belonging to the King. The citizens of London skated from bank to
bank of the river and even beyond where it had overflowed across the
low-lying fields of Chelsea and Lambeth, and they stopped to stare in
wonder at the fantastic costumes and furs of the ladies and gentlemen
behind the silken ropes. The ice was so thick, more than eight feet in
places, that fires could be built upon it, and salt was added to their
flames to make them burn with many colours. Booths selling all kinds
of goods, as well as hot, spiced drinks and gingerbread, were set up and
a roaring trade was done. The river was frozen right down to the

estuary, and even the sea was frozen around the coast. No ships were able to get into the port of London and, consequently, little trade was done and many of the poorer people were reduced to starvation level. Then, after a month or more had gone by, there was an ominous cracking sound, and the Court was just able to retreat in time into the Palace when the ice began to break up. But there were many who were not so fortunate, and they were swept away amidst the over-turned stalls and tumblers' booths, never to be seen again.

John Evelyn reported another such Frost Fair on 9 January 1684: 'I went across the Thames upon the ice, which was now become so incredibly thick as to bear not only whole streets of booths, in which they roasted meat and had divers shops of wares as in a town, but also coaches and carts and horses which passed over. So I went from Westminster Stairs to Lambeth and dined with my Lord Archbishop.

'The 24th. The frost still continuing more and more severe, the Thames before London was planted with booths in formal streets, as in a city or continual fair. All sorts of trades and shops were furnished and full of commodities – even to a printing press. . . . Coaches now plied from Westminster to the Temple, and from several other stairs to and fro as in the streets. There was likewise bull-baiting, horse and coach races, puppet plays and interludes, cooks and tippling – and lewder places – so that it seemed to be a bacchanalia, triumph, or carnival on the water. It was a severe judgement upon the land, for the trees were splitting as if lightning-struck, men and cattle perished in divers places, and the very seas were so locked up with ice that no vessels could stir out or come in.'

Cattle, fish and birds perished, and deer died in the game parks, so that there was a great shortage of food. Again the poor suffered, although there were various charitable contributions made to alleviate their lot. It was little comfort to the poor of London to learn that the cold was just as intense all over Europe, even in Spain and the far south.

ST BARTHOLOMEW'S FAIR...

Fairs had always been a favourite source of entertainment for the Londoner during the summer and autumn. One of the most important was St Bartholomew's Fair which was held for two days in August in West Smithfield in the parish of the saint. This fair was the setting for Ben Jonson's play of the same name. It sprang from medieval origins, and in those days was a fair for the sale of cloth imported from Flanders. But, since London now produced its own cloth which could be bought anywhere in the capital, there was no reason for a fair to sell just cloth alone. So its stalls began to display trinkets, cheap jewellery, food of all kinds, bright, cheap clothes and a special kind of gingerbread. Jugglers, tight-rope dancers and tumblers came into the fair from all over the country and abroad, and set up their booths. The noise was tremendous as the stallholders cried their wares and the 'barkers' shouted aloud the excellence of their performers. It was a paradise for the cut-purse, who would be hanged if caught, the quack doctor and the charlatan. As the century progressed, it was left more and more to the lower classes, and particularly to the apprentices. It was crowded, dirty, vulgar and extremely alive; and to the poor Londoner it was the event of the year. The opening was always attended by the Lord Mayor and his twelve Aldermen robed in their ceremonial scarlet and gold.

... AND OTHERS

There were other fairs whose original purpose had disappeared with time but which continued to exist simply for the sake of amusing the people; these were May Fair, held behind Piccadilly, which lasted for sixteen days in May, St James's Fair at the end of July, lasting three

Frontispiece by Wenceslas Hollar to 'Britannia', a Roadbook by John Ogilby 1675. Two well-to-do gentlemen, armed with one of the first roadbooks, pass through one of the City gates and set off in a northerly direction.

weeks, and Tothill Fair, in Westminster, in October. Most of these were banned and then allowed to continue after a certain space of time owing to disturbances caused by the rabble from time to time, but they brought a welcome note of celebration into the Londoner's life.

MASQUES

At the other end of the scale were the court masques which we have already mentioned with regard to the work of Inigo Jones. These elaborate, extravagant, often beautiful presentations were solely for the delight of the Court, and they existed during the first two Stuart reigns only. Perhaps to rival the Court entertainment, the City staged some magnificent pageants to celebrate the Lord Mayor's Show and employed writers and producers to create striking tableaux and little plays to be performed on pageant-carts in procession. Money was lavished on the Show and, on one occasion, the Grocers' Company spent nearly £900, which was a lot of money at that time.

HOLIDAYS

May Day, on the first of the month which had been dedicated to the Mother of God during earlier centuries, was still remembered, and people loved to go into the country on that day for picnics and to bring back wild flowers and garlands. This was the occasion when young men were allowed to escort their sweethearts – that being the accepted word for 'girl friend' – to a special meal either in one or the other's homes or in a family party at an inn. Everyone, male and female, kissed everybody else, it seems, during the seventeenth and eighteenth centuries: men meeting old friends would hug and kiss them as much as any footballer on the field does his team-mates today. St Valentine's Day was observed, with the exchange of presents, as was New Year's Day but, in the latter case, the lower orders made presents to their patrons, as an apprentice would to his master, the tenants to their noble landlords, and the nobility to the King, who was obviously the only one to gain by the custom. 20 November was still observed as Queen Elizabeth's Day, and there were processions and pagents until the time of the Commonwealth.

Of course, the Puritans did their best to suppress most of the Londoners' occasions of rejoicing: the Maypole was no longer raised in the City, and most of the other ancient customs were banned. But with the return of Charles II, many of the old celebrations were restored: people flocked once more to Hyde Park on May Day, and the milkmaids and chimney-sweeps, whose special day this was, had their processions once more but, unfortunately, most of the old dances were now forgotten. Pepys describes May Day in 1667: 'Up, it being a fine day, and after doing little business in my chamber to Westminster; in the way meeting many milkmaids with their garlands upon their pails, dancing with a fiddler before them; and saw pretty Nelly standing at her lodgings' door in Drury-lane in her smock sleeves and bodice, looking upon one: she seemed a mighty pretty creature.'

THE THEATRE

Pretty Nelly was, of course, Nell Gwynne, and she represented a great change which had taken place in the London theatre. Since the Restoration, women's roles were played by actresses and not by boys as they had been in the Elizabethan and Jacobean theatre. The exception to this had been the acting of the Queen and her ladies in the Court Masques, but these were never performed in public. On 8 December 1660 the first woman was seen on the stage of the theatre in Vere Street, in the part of Desdemona. On 3 January 1661 Pepys wrote in his diary: 'To the Theatre where was acted *Beggars' Bush*, it being very well done; and here the first time that ever I saw women come upon the stage.'

In 1642 the Puritan Parliament had closed the theatres; the old Elizabethan theatres of the Blackfriars and the Curtain had been closed down before the seventeenth century began, and the Roundheads had been responsible for the destruction or closing down of many more. When the law of 1657 was broken too often for the peace of the Puritan minds, another law was passed in 1647 giving powers of arrest during a performance. Most of the actors, such as Major Michael Mohun, left to join the Royalist forces and, later, the King in exile on the Continent.

In 1658, the year of Cromwell's death, William Davenant, the playwright, opened the Cockpit Theatre in Drury Lane for performances of the declamation of poetry and of music, but it was closed again in the following March. Davenant, or Sir William Davenant as he was to become, went over to Holland to join the King and came back in his train in May. Charles liked theatre-going and theatre people, and it was not very long after his return that he gave his patronage to Sir Thomas Killigrew's troop of actors known as the

A player's cart arriving at an inn. Frontispiece to 'A Comical Romance of a Company of Stage Players', an English translation of Scarron's 'Roman Comique'. Engraved by W. Fairhorne, 1676.

King's Servants, and they opened the King's Theatre. Sir William Davenant headed the troop under the patronage of the Duke of York and they played at the Duke's Theatre.

Shakespeare's work was still performed and revered, although some incredible things, such as putting a happy ending to *King Lear* were done in order to make the play easier to take for the vastly increasing numbers of the middle class. During Shakespeare's own time the groundlings who stood in the pit for a penny had taken the rough with the smooth, and were prepared to accept sad and unhappy things which held them as much enthralled as the clowns. Killigrew and Davenant wrote popular plays, and playwrights such as Sir John Vanburgh or John Dryden filled the theatres to capacity. In May 1663 Pepys tried to get into the Royal Theatre but it was so full he and his friends were turned away: 'And so to the Duke's house; and there saw *Hamlett* done, giving us fresh reason never to think enough of Betterton.' Thomas Betterton, the actor-manager and the Olivier of his day, was Pepys's favourite actor.

Performances began about 3.30 p.m. and ended about 6 p.m. and the plays were constantly changed. Oranges, nuts and ale were sold before the performance and during the intervals, and it was said that Nell Gwynne began her career in the theatre as an orange-seller. Some of the comedy was rough and vulgar and so ladies who had been taken to the

89

play wore masks to hide their blushes.

There had never been a theatre within the one square mile of the City, and there was no change with the Restoration, but there were many more theatres erected 'without the walls'. During Anne's reign, the Haymarket Opera House, which became known as the Queen's Theatre and later the King's Theatre, when the monarch changed, was opened in 1705 and lasted until it was burned down in 1789. Covent Garden Theatre was opened in 1709. Costumes for the more important actors and actresses were often passed on to them by even more important people: Charles II gave his coronation robes to Betterton and James II's queen, Mary of Modena, gave hers to an actress called Mrs Barry.

In spite of the affection and respect in which a number of actors and actresses were held by Charles II and other important people, they were still regarded as 'rogues and vagabonds'. When they died, they were still not allowed to be buried in consecrated ground, and while they lived their rights were few.

PARKS

There were still plenty of green spaces both within and outside London; Green Park and St James's Park had belonged formerly to the Abbey of Westminster until Henry VIII exchanged them for land he possessed at Hurley, Berkshire. Stocking them with deer, he put fences round them and turned them into royal hunting-grounds. In Cromwell's time Hyde Park became a place for driving around, and in Charles II's reign it became a fashionable promenade as well.

St James's Park began with Spring Gardens which were named after a spring rising from the ground there. There were lawns, fruit-trees, bowling greens and archery butts, all of which belonged to the King, but he gave his permission for the public to use them. An ordinary, or eating-house, was opened there during Charles I's reign, but after a number of brawls the gardens were partly closed. In 1654 they were closed entirely and remained so for four years. When they were reopened they lost their original popularity and people turned to the New Spring Gardens at Vauxhall, to walk among the flowerbeds. Pepys and his friend, Mr Creed, took a boat to Vauxhall on a warm May evening and found that 'it is very pleasant and cheap going thither, for a man may go to spend what he will, or nothing, all is one. But to hear the nightingale and other birds, and here fiddles, and there a harp, and here a Jew's trump, and here laughing, and there fine people walking, is mighty diverting.'

There were other green spaces in Moorfields, where the archery butts had been in Elizabeth's time, in Hoxton Fields and Spa Fields in Clerkenwell; within a quarter of an hour you could walk from any part of the City and find yourself in fields. For people living in Holborn and Fleet Street, Gray's Inn Fields or Lamb's Conduit Fields were quiet retreats from the bustle of the town.

Late seventeenth-century sword-hilts ornamented with gold wire and silver filigree.

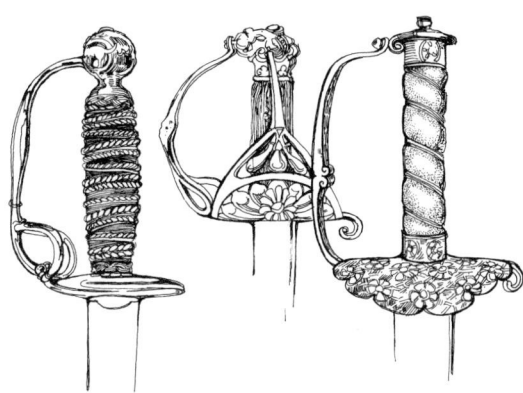

SPORT AND ENTERTAINMENT

When the Puritans stopped public games on Sunday, the working-man's only day for rest and recreation, they prevented him for eighteen years from playing bowls, ringing bells, shooting or wrestling. The result was that the lower classes lost their old agility and quickness of eye, and their only amusements were to drift around in rabbles which were quickly inflamed by drink or demagogues.

During the winter, the wealthier people amused themselves indoors with cards, dice and games of chance of all kinds: gambling was rife and large sums were won and lost in a night at Court and elsewhere. They also played chess, shuttlecock and billiards and, out of doors, they skated on the frozen ponds. In summer, there were swimming, riding and tennis, and fencing and dancing the whole year round. After the Restoration, bull- and bear-baiting were revived, but their popularity had waned in the interval. Pepys described bear-baiting as 'a very rude and nasty pleasure.' But, lest we should think that the middle- and upper-class Londoners had at last reached a new height of compassion and civilization, we should also remember that the same people regarded a public hanging as an occasion for an entertaining morning or afternoon out.

A whole new class had arisen in London. These were the fashionable people who all lived in the same part of London in fine houses which they had built for themselves. They were to be seen in the same coffee-houses and the same theatres; they all followed the same kind of life based on amusement, and they developed their own fashionable 'language'. Politics was a game to them, and gambling a most serious study: the only time they really liked leaving London for the country was when they set out for horseracing at Newmarket. They formed their own 'set' and were careful to marry within it. This was the beginning of 'society' as it has been called ever since.

Against this type of Londoner can be balanced the enquiring minds of those learned and often professional men who formed the Royal Society established by Charles II at the beginning of his reign, although its nucleus had existed since about 1645. Its full title was The Royal Society for Improving Natural Knowledge, and many subjects were discussed and papers read about physics, chemistry and natural philosophy. Men such as Christopher Wren and Robert Boyle were honoured members, and both Pepys and Evelyn were elected Presidents. This was the Golden Age which produced architects such as Wren, Vanburgh and Hawksmoor, writers of the quality of Addison, Dryden and Swift, and philosophers such as Hobbes and Locke.

The old, picturesque quality of Tudor London had almost vanished, but a city was arising which, although it was not perfect, reflected the new spirit of the times. The men of enquiring minds were always ready to experiment, and this can be seen from Wren's work alone; few architects have worked with such perfect confidence in so many different styles. Although, unfortunately, the City of London could not be planned as a whole, its new buildings had a kind of orderliness about them which had never been seen in the capital before. And, as a new light of scientific reasoning was being applied to most branches of learning, it seemed symbolic that the streets of the new London were wider, the houses loftier and the windows larger to let in more light.

Select Bibliography

The Cities of London and Westminster NIKOLAUS PEVSNER Penguin

London, the Biography of a City CHRISTOPHER HIBBERT Longmans

London Fabric JAMES POPE-HENNESSY Batsford

A Concise History of Costume JAMES LAVER Thames & Hudson

The Observer's Book of European Costume GEOFFREY SQUIRE AND PAULINE BAYNES Frederick Warne & Co.

London's Burning JOHN BEDFORD Abelard-Schuman

Discovering London 5: Stuart London MALPAS PEARSE Macdonald

London's Riverside SUZANNE EBEL AND DOREEN IMPEY William Luscombe Ltd

London in the time of the Stuarts SIR WALTER BESANT Chatto & Windus

The Diary of John Evelyn

The Diary of Samuel Pepys

Samuel Pepys, 3 vols SIR ARTHUR BRYANT Cambridge

Restoration England SIR ARTHUR BRYANT Collins

Pepys RICHARD OLLARD Hodder & Stoughton

Sir Christopher Wren SIR JOHN SUMMERSON Pelican

The London Nobody Knows GEOFFREY FLETCHER Hutchinson

Nairn's London IAN NAIRN Penguin

Index

Addison, Joseph 79, 81, 82, 92
Aldermen 16, 30, 60, 85
Allen, Dr. 79
Almack's 81
Alsatia 28
Anne of Denmark 8, 13, 14
Anne, Queen 61, 63, 64, 81, 90
apprentices 71
Archer, Thomas 81
Arundel, Earl of 11
Arundel House *11*

Bailey, Captain 51
Bank of England 63
Banqueting House, Whitehall 10, 14, 21, 53
Barbon, Dr Nicholas 57–9
Barry, Mrs 90
Bear Garden, the 23
Beaufort House 15
Bedford, Francis Russell, 4th Earl of 11, 56
Bedford House 13, 57
Bedford Row 57
Bedford Street 57
Beefsteak Club 81
Bernini 42
Betterton, Thomas 89, 90
Billingsgate 39, 49
Blackfriars 39, 41
Blackfriars Theatre 88
Bloomsbury 13, 18, 56, 57, 64
Bloomsbury Square 56
Boodles Club 81
Bordes, Mme de 44
Bourne, Nicholas 81
Boyle, Robert 92
Bramante 45
British coffee-house, the 80
Brooke's Club 81
Buckingham, Duke of 15, 20, 51
Burlington, Earl of 15
Burlington House 56
Butter, Nathaniel 81
Button's Coffee-house 80

Cannon Street 34
'Change Alley 79
Chapter Coffee-house, the 80
Charles I, King 8, 14, 20, *21*, 38, 40, 42, 77, 82
Charles II, King 23, 26, 32, 34, 36, *37*, 40, 43–5, 47, 53, 54, 56, 58, 60, 61, 64, 69, 88, 90, 92
Charterhouse 52
Cheapside 59, 75
Chelsea 83
Child, Sir Francis 59
Child's Bank 59

Chiswick, Earl of Burlington's Villa at 15
chocolate-houses 80
Churches:
    All Hallows the Great 31
    All Hallows the Less 31
    Christchurch in Spitalfields 34, 61
    St Alphege, Greenwich 61
    St Andrew by the Wardrobe 42
    St Andrew, Holborn 29
    St Anne, Limehouse 61
    St Benet 42, 43
    St Bartholomew the Great 8, 52
    St Clement Dane 29
    St Clement in Eastcheap 42
    St Dunstan in the West 34
    St Edmund King and Martyr 42
    St Faith 36
    St George, Bloomsbury 61
    St George in the East 61
    St Giles in the Fields 29
    St James, Piccadilly 54
    St Katherine by the Tower 52
    St Lawrence Jewry 42
    St Magnus the Martyr 31
    St Martin in the Fields 29
    St Mary Aldermary 42
    St Mary-le-Bow 42
    St Mary Woolnoth 61
    St Olave 30
    St Paul's Cathedral 15, 34, *35*, 38, 41, 44, 45, 46, 64, 81, 82
    St Paul, Covent Garden 11
City Companies 37
City Halls 34
City Walls 52, 54
Clarendon, Earl of 55
Clarendon House 55
Clerkenwell 22, 28
Clothmakers, Company of 16
Clubs 80
coal tax 40, 41
Cockpit Theatre, the 88
Cocoa-Tree Coffee-house, the 80
coffee-houses 78, 79, 80, 81
communications 74, 75
Compton, Sir Francis 57
Cornhill 9, 34, 79
Covent Garden 11, 15, 18, 54, 59, 60
Covent Garden Theatre 90
Coventry, Sir William 37
Cromwell 8, 22, 23, 40, 51, 52, 53, 88
Cripplegate 52
Crutched Friars 52
Curtain Theatre 88

Davenant, Sir William 88, 89

Defoe, Daniel 82
Deptford 47
docks and wharves 48
Dockwra, William 75
Dowgate 28
Drake, Sir Francis 18
drink 74
Drury Lane 88
Dryden, John 79, 89, 92
Duke Street 54
Duke's Theatre 89
Durham House 9

Eastcheap 34
East India Company 49
East India Dock 49
Elizabeth I, Queen 7, 9, 15, 18, 27, 34, 91
Elizabeth, Princess Palatine 52
entertainment 91
Essex House 58
Evelyn, John 13, 26, 33, 34, 36, 38, 43, 46, 92

Farynor, or Farriner, Thomas 31
Farringdon Street 41
Fish Street Hill 31, 45
Fleet Canal, the 41
Fleet Street 28, 36, 59, 91
food 74, 77
Fortune Theatre, the 23
Frost fairs 83, 84
furniture 72, 73

Gibbons, Grinling 43, 44, 54
Globe Theatre, the 23
Glorious Revolution, the 43
Gloucester, Duke of 40
Gracechurch Street 34
Gray's Inn 59
Gray's Inn Fields 71
Gray's Inn Road 28
Greater London 40, 47
Great Fire, the 23, 39, 41, 45, 46, 49, 53, 64,
   70
Great Hurricane, the 62
Great Russell Street 51
Greenland Docks 49
Green Park 90
Greenwich, Royal Hospital 43, 61
Gresham, Sir Thomas 9
Grocers' Company 87
Grocers' Hall 63
Guildhall, the 41
Gwynne, Nell 59, 88, 89

hackney-coaches 51
Hamlet 89
Hampstead 38
Hampton Court 61
Hawksmoor, Nicholas 43, 61, 64, 92
Henrietta Maria, Queen 14, 44, 53
Henry VIII, King 28, 90
Henry, Prince of Wales 10, *12*, 16, 77
Highgate 34
Hobbes, Thomas 92
Holborn 41, 91
Holborn Viaduct 41
holidays 87
household, the 75

houses 72
Howland's Dock 49
Hoxton Fields 91
Hyde Park 88

Isle of Dogs 30
Islington 34, 38

Jacobites, the 80
James I 8, 14–16, *17*, 18, 19, 23, 40, 52, 77, 83
James II 53, 61, 63, 64
Jermyn, Henry, Earl of St Albans 53, 54
Jermyn Street 54
Johnson, Ben 9, 85
Jones, Inigo 7–15, 34, 42, 87

Kensington 13, 18, 38
Kensington Palace 53, 61
Killigrew, Sir Thomas 88, 89
King's Theatre 89, 90
King Street, St James 54
Kit Kat Club 81
Knightsbridge 38, 54, 64
Knights Hospitallers of the Order of St
   John 52

Lambeth 30, 83
Lamb's Conduit Fields 91
Laud, William, Bishop of London 20
Leaden Hall 60
Lincoln's Inn 65
Lloyd's Coffee-house 79
Locke, John 92
Lockett's Tavern 78
Lombard Street 40
London Bridge 18, 28, 49, 50, 51
London, Pool of 40, 48, 49
London, Port of 40
Lord Mayor 16, 31, 32, 60, 85
Lord Mayor's Show 87
Louis XIV 42, 47, 56
Louvre, the 42
Ludgate 36
Ludgate Hill 75

Macclesfield, Earl of 57
main roads 78
Mall, the 55
Mansard 42
Mary II, Queen 43, 52, 59, 61, 63, 64
Mary of Modena, Queen of James II 11, 90
Masques 9, 87, 88
May Day 87, 88
May Fair 85
Maypole, the 23, 87
men's clothes 69, 70
Merchant Taylor's Company 16
middle classes, the new 64, 65
Millwall 49
Minories, the 30
Mint, the Royal 57
Mohun, Major Michael 88
Monmouth, Duke of 57
Monmouth Street 70
Monument, the 41, 45, 46, 64
Moorfields 91
Morrice, Peter 18

Myddleton, Sir Hugh *18*, 19

Nando's Coffee-house 80
National Debt 63
Neale, Thomas 57
Newgate 60
New Exchange 9, 37, *41*, 59, 60, 75
New River 18, 19
newspapers 81
Nottingham, Earl of 61

Olimpico, Teatro, at Vicenza 7, 8

Pall Mall 54, 55, 64
Palladio, Andrea 7, 10
Parks 90
Parliament 20, 40, 61, 88
Paul's Wharf 36, 42
Penn, Sir William 65
Pepys, Samuel 30, 32, *33*, 43, 49, 50, 65, 72, 73, 74, 78, 88, 89, 90, 91, 92
Phoenix Life Insurance 58
Piccadilly 54, 55, 65
Plague, the Great 27, *29*, 30, 31
Plymouth 30
poor, the 70
Prince Palatine, the 52
Pudding Lane 31, 45
Puritans 20, 53, 91

Queen Elizabeth's Day 87
Queen's Chapel, St James 14
Queen's House, Greenwich *13*, 14
Queen's Theatre, the 90

Red Lion Fields 58
Red Lion Square 65
Regent's Canal 30
Restoration, the 23, 52, 53, 90
Roos, Lord 7
Rose Tavern, the 78
Rose Theatre, the 23
Rotherhithe 47, 49
Royal Exchange 9, 21, 34, 38, 41, *42*, 60, 75, 79
Royal Society 92
Royal Theatre, the 89
Rubens, Peter Paul 14, 21
Rupert, Prince of the Rhine 59
Russell Street 57
Rutland, Earl of 8

St Bartholomew's Fair 85
St Giles's Coffee-house 89
St James, quarter of 64
St James's Coffee-house 80
St James's Fair 85
St James's Fields 54
St James's Market 60
St James's Park 64, 70
St James's Square 54
St James's Street 54, 81
St Paul's School 36
St Peter's, Rome 45
St Valentine's Day 87
Salisbury, Earl of 9
Sayes Court, Deptford 43
sedan-chairs 51

Seething Lane 30, 73
sewers 40
Shakespeare 56, 89
Ship Money 20, 40
shops 75
Smyrna Coffee-house 80
society 92
Soho Fields 38
Soho Square 57
Southampton, Earl of 56
Southampton House 57
Southampton Street 57
Southampton Row 57
Southwark 52
Spa Fields, Clerkenwell 91
Spitalfields 47, 56, 58, 65
sport 90
Spring Gardens 90
Steele, Sir Richard 79, 82
Stock Exchange 79
Stow, John 7, 51
Storm, the Great 62, 63
Strand, the 57, 58, 59, 75
Sun Tavern, the 78
Surrey Docks, the 49
Swan Theatre, the 23
Swift, Jonathan 79, 92

taverns 78
Taylor, John 52
Temple, the 37
Thames, the river 28, 29, 32, 41, 50, 52, 60
Thames Street 18, 31
Thatched House Tavern 81
theatres 88, 89
Tintoretto 43
Tonnage and Poundage 40
Tories 80
Tothill Fair 87
trade 47
Tower of London, the 30, 33, 49
Tower Hamlets 27

Vanburgh, Sir John 43, 64, 81, 92
Vauxhall 90

Walpole, Sir Robert 81
Watchmen 52
weather 83
Westminster 18, 28, 29
Westminster Abbey 63
West Smithfield 52, 85
Whigs 80
Whitechapel 47, 65
White Friars 28
Whitehall *10*, 18, 30, 32, 37, 53
White's Club 81
wigs 65, 66
William, Prince of Orange, King William III 43, 53, 57, 61, 63, 64
Will's Coffee-house 79, 80
women's clothes 67, 68
Wren, Sir Christopher 38, 41, 43, 44, 45, 46, 54, 61, 64, 92

York, Duke of 32, 34, 40, 65, 75, 89
York House 15